(join)

our club

This is your own personal Smith membership card. The moment you register it online you will start receiving details of exclusive last-minute offers from the hotels featured, and lots more. The Smith card provides members-only privileges at all of o... such as a free bottle of champagne on arriv... upgrades, discounts on room rates – just... when you book, and show your card at che...

Look out for the **Smith** at the end of each review.

Activate your card today by registering online at www.mrandmrssmith.com. (It only takes a minute.)

A *Mr & Mrs Smith* membership card should be affixed here.
If it has been removed, you can still buy the book and we will send you a replacement card. Please send proof of purchase, with a return address, to
Spy Publishing Ltd
192–194 Clapham High Street
London SW4 7UD
United Kingdom

Register now

Activate your membership today and you will receive our newsletter, the Guest Book; it's packed with news, tips, offers, and competitions. We promise not to bombard you with communications, or pass on details to third parties; this is strictly between you and us.

ente

There are some wonderful places to stay out there, if you know where to find them. It's fine to have high expectations – so long as the experience lives up to them. Mr & Mrs Smith guides you around the UK and Ireland's most stylish and individual hotels. From which room or suite to ask for, to where best to have Sunday lunch, this is the inside story. And to make it even easier for all of your dreams to come true, we have created an online booking service at www.mrandmrssmith.com.

Whether you're looking for a quirky boutique hotel, a deluxe retreat or simply a great pub, we've chosen destinations to suit all budgets and moods. We have even researched what's going on around each hotel so you can make the most of your time there... should you make it out of bed.

All our reviews have been carried out anonymously. Each contributor tells his or her own tale, evoking the spirit of the place and giving a recommendation you can trust. We also have an exclusive membership scheme, so remember to register your Smith card when booking, to take advantage of the great offers now available to you.

We had to kiss a lot of frogs to bring you this prince. Having shortlisted 150 hotels from more than 1,000 candidates, we hope you have fun working your way through the final 41 that made the collection. From now on, may all your hotel experiences have a very happy ending.

Mr & Mrs Smith

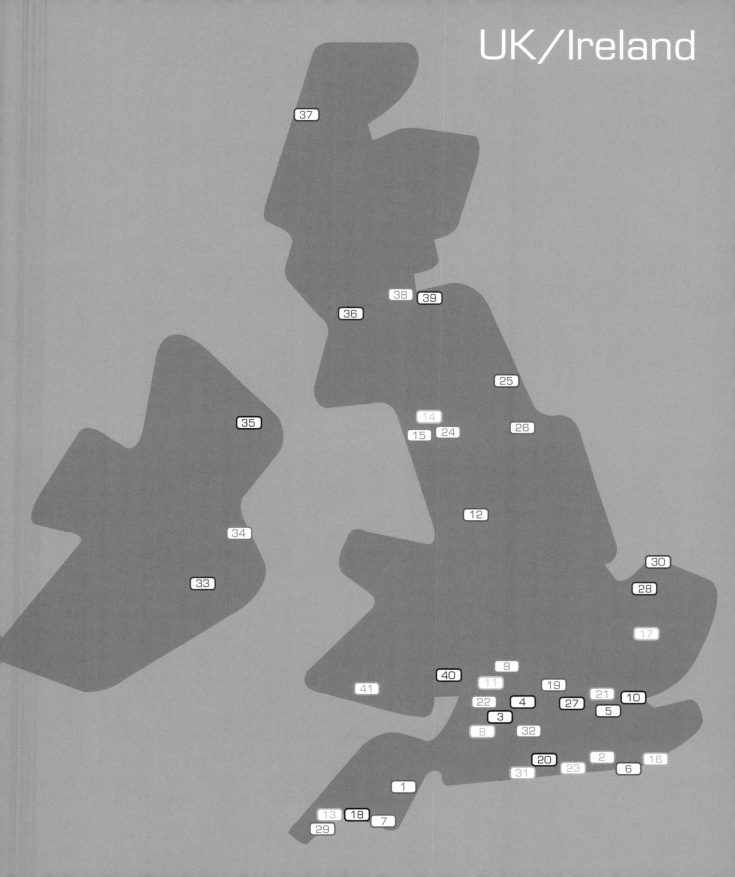

UK/Ireland

(at a glance)

Scotland

Ireland

Wales

England

Alias Hotel Barcelona

M T W T F ◼ M T W T F S S M T W T F S S M T W T F S S M T W T F S S M

Style Young and quirky
Setting Exeter Central

TWTFSSMTWTFSSMTWTFSSMTWTFSSMTWTFSSMTWTFSSM

the interior is a far cry from the hotel's past

It's not often you're hit on the head by a flying rubber glove as you walk down the high street. And it's not every morning you wake up and find yourself in a double bed in an eye hospital. These may sound like scenes from the mind of David Cronenberg, but actually they're flashbacks to our weekend in Devon.

From the outside, there's no mistaking Barcelona's previous incarnation. But the warm glow of a chandelier in the lobby signals that the interior is a far cry from the hotel's past; after all, this is the place that won Design Hotel of the Year 2002. If you're a lover of Ian Schrager-style mismatched furniture, but not such a fan of his price-tags, Alias Hotels have you in mind. The venetian mirrors and retro furniture in reception told us this was a place with a personality and the young, friendly staff signalled that it was relaxed and cost-conscious. Once we were checked in, it was up the stairs, past a dentist's chair, and down the hallway to our home for the weekend. Not built to be a hotel, Barcelona has rooms in every shape and size. We'd requested the largest room available, preferably overlooking the garden and not the busy road out front, which made all the difference.

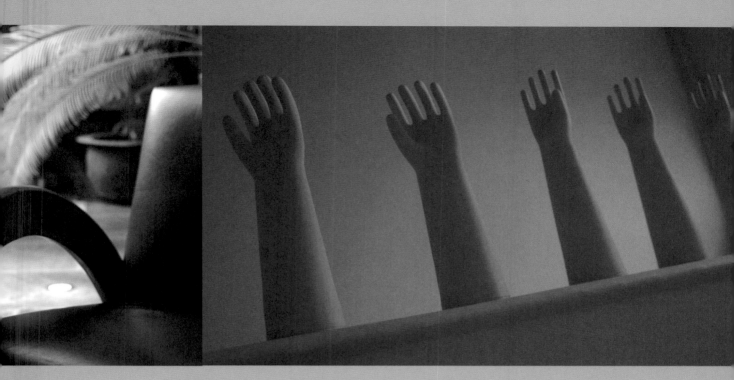

The hotel is located a credit card's throw from the centre of Exeter so, it being a Saturday, we slung our luggage onto the enormous bed and headed off for a little shopping, through the postcard-perfect Cathedral Square, over the High Street and down to cobblestoned Gandy Street. A pair of Seven jeans and a DKNY jumper later, we were strolling back to base when the rubber glove from above struck. With the sun past the yard-arm, we took it as a slap from the tequila gods to head straight to the hotel bar, Kino, to try one of Barcelona's legendary margaritas.

Early evening and the bar was buzzing: hotel guests and locals were bagsying the best seats in the adjoining club to catch that night's jazz band. However, by then, we were more in search of sustenance than a party. Café Paradiso, upstairs, is as crucial a part of Exeter nightlife as Kino, attracting dressed-up couples and groups of friends, some young, some older and wiser, all in good spirits. The Mediterranean cuisine is ambitious, expertly executed and exceedingly good value, so it's always packed. After dinner, although the sounds of the packed bar below wafted up enticingly, we chose to have a few more drinks in the more low-key surrounds of the lounge. At half past ten, it was empty but for a fellow slumped on his own on the sofa; it turned out to be Uri Geller mourning Exeter FC's relegation. Resisting the temptation to ask him if he was on some sort of bender, we left him to sleep away his sorrows and ordered a nightcap to take up to our room.

If you do indulge in one too many cocktails in Kino, Barcelona couldn't offer more in the way of balm for the morning after the night before. What the power showers in the bright bathrooms can't wash away, breakfast in the sunny conservatory soon knocks into touch. Feeling whole again, we set off to explore the nearby quay. This time, our outing didn't include any gloves falling from the sky – just a ferry ride to a pub along the canal. Anything that inspires the words 'it's not often you get to...' is surely an opportunity not to be missed. Like staying in a converted medical institution. Or an encounter with the most ingenious waterbombs in the south-west. And hey, Exeter may not be Manhattan, but Hotel Barcelona makes up for that by having all the energy of the city it's named after.

Reviewed by Mr & Mrs Smith

Need to know

Rooms 46.
Rates £85–£125.
Check-out 11am.
Facilities Beauty treatments can be arranged in advance.
Kids Childcare can be arranged.

In the know

Recommended rooms Rooms vary in size; specify a large one. Ask for a view over the Victorian walled garden. The unique Theatre Room is an old operating theatre.
Packing tips VHS videos, CDs.
Also The Alias Group includes Kandinsky in Cheltenham, Rossetti in Manchester, Seattle in Brighton; visit www.aliashotels.com for details.

Food & drink

In the hotel Café Paradiso serves international brasserie food, and has a wood-burning pizza oven. Kino, the cocktail bar, is buzzing in the evening.
Dress code Anything goes.
Top table Ask for a garden view.
Last orders Food: 9.45pm; 8.45pm on a Sunday. Kino: 1am during the week; 1.30am Friday and Saturday; closed on Sundays.
Room service 24 hours.
Breakfast 7am–10am; until 10.30am at weekends.
Local restaurants **Michael Caines** at the Royal Clarence Hotel (01392 310031) has two Michelin stars. **Brazz** (01392 252525) does an excellent brunch. In Taunton, the **Castle Hotel** (01823 272671) has a Michelin star and is a great fine-dining experience.
Local pubs The **Jack in the Green** (01404 822240) in Rockbeare is a great gastropub. Otherwise, catch a ferry from the quay to **Double Locks Pub** (01392 256947) for a pint.

Worth getting out of bed for

Saddles and Paddles (01392 424241; www.saddlepaddle.co.uk). Exe Power Boat and Ski Club, Exmouth (01395 267673) provides powerboating, wakeboarding and waterskiing half an hour's drive away. In Exeter, you'll find designer clothes from Willys on Gandy Street, and vintage at Real McCoy; Eclectique down on the quay is great for antique knick-knacks.
Diary July: Exeter Festival (01392 213161; www.exeter.gov.uk/festival) for theatre, Proms in the Park, comedy and fireworks; Exmouth Grand Prix – powerboat racing (www.rya. org.uk/powerboating). August: Dartmouth Royal Regatta (www.dartmouthregatta.co.uk).

Smith A copy of the *Café Paradiso Cookbook*.

Get a room! Check availability and make reservations through www.mrandmrssmith.com.

Alias Hotel Barcelona Magdalen Street, Exeter (01392 281000)
info@aliasbarcelona.com; www.aliashotels.com

Amberley Castle

M T W T F ▢ M T W T F S S M T W T F S S M T W T F S S M

Style Moated mediaeval retreat
Setting Scenic Sussex

Amberley

T F S S M T W T F S S M T W T F S S M T W T F S S M T W T

it was so filmic we looked around for
someone with a remote control

As we drove up the gravel drive, with the sun sinking to the left in a cloudless sky, a flock of what looked like doves soared across the meadows in front and swooped up over the ramparts. It was so filmic we looked around for someone with a remote control orchestrating it all. We felt suitably period-drama as we arrived at the main gates and swept under the portcullis, ending the scene perfectly.

One of the super-friendly but not in-your-face staff greeted us and pointed us to the reception. We were then politely shown to our room and left to get on with it. It was extremely cosy, with a comfortable sofa, inglenook and voluminous drape above the bed, and once we had consigned a gaggle of cuddly toys to the wardrobe, we were able to spread out and unwind. The Jacuzzi was particularly instrumental in the relaxation scenario, helped along by a selection of delicious-smelling Floris products.

I will confess that I usually have a niggling prejudice against this kind of establishment. When it comes to fitting out English castles as hotels, I can't help but line up on the side of Mies van der Rohe and his modernist edict, 'less is more'. The consensus usually appears to be that the more chintzy decoration and furniture you can stuff in, the more authentic and comfortable it will seem. (And if you need a crowbar to get a bit more in, then use it.) However, as we settled into our room, Camber (all are named after Sussex castles), I softened. Even those with a taste for Hempel-like restraint will be appeased by the historical setting, good taste of the furnishings and Amberley's incredible grounds.

Windy weather put paid to the game of tennis we'd hoped for, but we were actually starting to feel too relaxed to exert ourselves, and happily settled for a leisurely stroll around the ramparts. The signs warning us to proceed at our own risk were not enough to dissuade us from climbing the rickety stairs, and we made it to the top of the tower just in time to watch the sun sink below the South Downs. Here, we discovered the bird coops that seemed to explain the multitude of swans, peacocks, pigeons (and the obligatory rooks) that, though not remote controlled, seemed to know when they were needed for a spot of scene-setting.

There is no bar as such in Amberley Castle; drinks are brought to you in one of three adjacent sitting rooms. As our wanderings had made us late, we skipped a pre-prandial tipple and went straight in for supper. The whole feel of the Queen's Room is that of a well-appointed rural French restaurant (it helps that the entire waiting staff are from over the Channel). The only clue that we were in Blighty was the inclusion of an English bottle in an extensive wine bible that arrived as we sat down. The menu was extremely tempting, and we both chose well – I had a main course of deliciously tender venison, which I would rate as probably the best I've ever eaten.

Each of the lounges has a particular atmosphere, and we thought we'd take our coffee in one of the quieter rooms. But everyone else had crowded into the library with its deep sofas and blazing fire, and it looked so convivial that we ended up squeezing in with the other guests. When we got the chance, we pounced on the opportunity to take up pole position in front of the fire. Here we stayed, chatting, for a couple of hours longer. If we were keeping the staff up later than usual, they were so polite and discreet they never let on. Our evening could only have been bettered if it had been occupied with plans for exploring the area the next day. Alas, try as we might to figure out a way to stay longer, a phone call from work put an end to our hopes. Still, at least we knew that 900-year-old Amberley would, very likely, still be there next time we passed this way.

Reviewed by Anthony Thistleton

Need to know

Rooms 19.
Rates £155–£374.
Check-out 11am.
Facilities 12 acres of grounds, including an 18-hole putting course, tennis court, croquet.
Kids Over-12s welcome.
Also No smoking in the dining room or bedrooms.

In the know

Recommended rooms Try and stay in the main body of the castle. Amberley has a sumptuous bed, his 'n' hers bathrooms and a window-seat looking over the courtyard. Pevensey is intimate and has its own private door leading to the castle battlements.
Packing tips Camera, book of ghost stories, tennis racket.
Also Two-night minimum stay at the weekend. A sister hotel is opening in Burgundy in 2006.

Food & drink

In the hotel Traditional British menu with contemporary influences.
Dress code No denim, even at lunchtime; jacket or tie for dinner.
Top table In the window alcove.
Last orders Food: 9.30pm. Bar: normal licensing hours.
Room service Until 9.30pm.
Breakfast 7.30am–10am.
Local pubs The **Royal Oak** in Lavant (01243 527434; see page 156) is worth the trip for lunch, as is the **Black Horse** in Amberley Village (01798 831552). The **George and Dragon Inn** in Houghton (01903 883131) has delicious bar food as well as a restaurant.

Worth getting out of bed for

Archery, clay-pigeon shooting and hot-air ballooning can be arranged by the hotel. Goodwood House (www.goodwood.co.uk) – you can have helicopter and flying lessons at the Flying Club, go to the races or watch the motor-racing. While you're there, walk up Trundle Lane to the Seven Points Viewpoint. Chichester Festival Theatre (www.cft.org.uk) puts on impressive productions. The Minerva Theatre (01243 781312) next door, has fringe-type performances. Have a stroll along Climping beach, a ten-minute drive away.
Diary May–August: Glyndebourne Festival Opera (01273 813813; www.glyndebourne.com).
June: Polo British Open Championships at Cowdray Park (01730 813257; www.cowdraypolo.co.uk).
July: Festival of Speed and Glorious Goodwood (01243 755055; www.goodwood.co.uk).

Smith A special-edition book celebrating Amberley Castle's 900th year.

Get a room! Check availability and make reservations through www.mrandmrssmith.com.

Amberley Castle Amberley, near Arundel, West Sussex (01798 831992)
info@amberleycastle.co.uk; www.amberleycastle.co.uk

Babington House

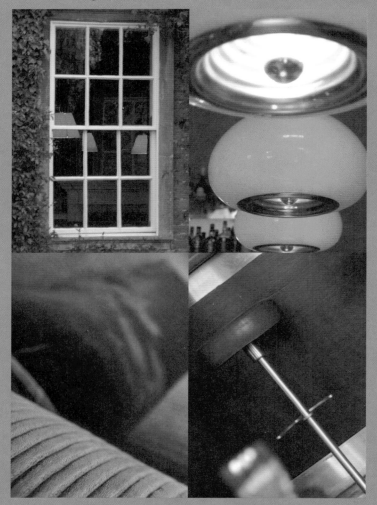

MTWTFSSMTWTF █ MTWTFSSMTWTFSSMTWTFSSM

Style Relaxed retro country club
Setting Deepest Somerset

the shabby-chic decor is effortlessly cool

Babington House certainly has a lot of ardent fans; trying to book a room there is about as easy as booking a table for two at the Ivy. It's worth it, though. We knew before we went what the country cousin of major media hang-out Soho House is trying to achieve – its launch in 1998 famously kick-started the march of metropolitan cool into the countryside – and we hoped the reality was going to live up to the fantasy. As we drove up the classic long driveway, our destination appeared just how we had imagined: an impressive manor-house and chapel, in rolling grounds. It was only when we spotted the enormous double hammocks swinging here and there that we realised this was a stately with a difference.

Hip staff, wisely plucked from London operations, greeted us at the door, not a uniform in sight. Our car was whisked away while we were shown around, the staff making sure we knew that, here, anything goes. The truly relaxing do-what-you-want atmosphere is Babington's real feat; others can imitate, but it's the service that makes the difference. That and the scale of the place. All the rooms are massive – ours had a thrillingly huge bed, a bath big enough for two alongside it, and a TV resembling a small

cinema screen. After an hour's bathing, using as much
of their Cowshed (the name of the spa – there's
a bit of a cattle theme going on) products as we possibly
could, it was time to get done up and get downstairs.

There's no dress code for supper – whether you turn
up barefoot or doll up glam, you'll feel equally comfortable.
That's what makes Babington so clever. We walked into the
bar, and forgot we were in the countryside. We might have
been back in London, had it been a bit more hectic. A
flickering 'golf ball' chandelier, retro lights over the bar, and
comfy sofas in leather, suede and cord complete the look.
The barman knew his cocktails and we settled in to a
couple of Cosmopolitans, but it's just as perfect for a pint,
cosy, firelit and friendly. Upstairs is the new and rather
sexy 'grown-ups only' Martini Bar.

We set off to the Log Room for dinner. Just as you can
wear what you want here, you can eat what you fancy.
The menu has everything from pizzas and pies to caviar
and full à la carte – strange, but it works. The food and
service were excellent, and after a bottle of wine we were
fully into the Babington way of life. When we arrived back
at our room, two little pots of balm had been delivered by

the BH fairy, the labels reading 'Sleepy Cow' and 'Raging Bull'. Having spent several hours in the bar, I can't remember which we went for – but we did sleep well...

The next day, after a particularly well-appointed fruit salad for breakfast, we embraced the champagne-hippie vibe of the hotel. A morning swim in the spectacular outdoor pool – built on the brow of a hill so you feel as though you're floating in the middle of all that green – was followed by a massage in the random teepee by the lake and the ducks. There were quite a few children running around, but there's no chance of them getting on anyone's nerves; they are supremely catered for with their own 'Little House' next to the spa. Feeling much better, we went off to explore the beautiful countryside and have lunch at a fantastic local pub, the Talbot in Mells.

More of the same led us to the end of a supremely chilled-out weekend. So, did it live up to our expectations? In a word, yes. The atmosphere at Babington is as laidback as the shabby-chic decor is effortlessly cool. The media crowd have retreated slightly, but the sophisticated and super-welcoming vibe remains. In terms of home-from-home havens for spoilt urbanites, this, in our humble opinion, is still the daddy.

Reviewed by Mr & Mrs Smith

Need to know

Rooms 28 rooms, from suites to split-level mini-houses ideal for families.
Rates £215–£370 (Babington/Soho House members: £180–£335).
Check-out Midday, but once you've checked out you can hang around.
Facilities Indoor and outdoor pools, gym and Cowshed spa, DVD and CD libraries, billiards,
45-seat cinema, croquet lawn, tennis courts, cricket pitch.
Kids Very welcome: the Little House is a creche. Babysitting can also be arranged.

In the know

Recommended rooms We loved sexy Room 5, with a free-standing bath by the bed;
Room 6, with its Jacuzzi on a private terrace; and Room 12 for its eight-foot bed and
big bathroom with views to the lake. For weekends, book six months ahead.
Packing tips Don't forget your swimsuit (though there's a shop if you do), goggles,
and suitable attire to walk from bedroom to spa.
Also Wellies provided.

Food & drink

In the hotel There are three dining areas: the Breakfast Room, the Log Room, and the terrace.
There's also a bar on the ground floor and the child-free Martini Bar on the first floor.
Dress code Barefoot or ballgown.
Top table At the back of the Log Room, away from the kitchen.
Last orders The restaurant closes when last guest leaves. Bar open until 2am, later for residents.
Room service Anything, any time.
Breakfast Served all day from 7am in House Kitchen.
Local restaurants The Michelin-starred **Moody Goose** in Bath (01225 466688).
The **Moon and Sixpence** (01225 460962) is relaxed and informal, with good modern food.
Local pubs The **Talbot Inn** in Mells (01373 812254) serves game. The **Angel Inn** in Hindon
(01747 820696) serves amazing fish (closed Sunday evenings). The **Black Dog**
in Chilmark (01722 716344) does both contemporary and traditional food. The **Beckford
Arms** in Fonthil Gifford (01747 870385) is good for a pint.

Worth getting out of bed for

Horse-riding and clay-pigeon shooting in Wellow (01225 834376). Ballooning (0870 607
0241). Golf in Frome (01373 454200). Longleat has numerous attractions which include the
house, safari park and a butterfly garden (01985 844328; www.longleat.co.uk).
Diary August: hot-air-balloon festival, Bristol (0117 953 5884; www.bristolfiesta.co.uk).
Glastonbury Classical Festival offers the more sedate side of the musical spectrum (01458
832020; www.glastonburyfestivals.co.uk/classical).

Smith A complimentary bottle of Horny Cow Seductive Bath & Massage Oil.

Get a room! Check availability and make reservations through www.mrandmrssmith.com.

Babington House Babington, near Frome, Somerset (01373 812266)
enquiries@babingtonhouse.co.uk; www.babingtonhouse.co.uk

Barnsley House

MTWTF ■ MTWTFSSMTWTFSSMTWTFSS

Style Super-stylish manor-house
Setting Gorgeous Gloucestershire gardens

WTF**SS**MTWTFSSMTWTFSSMTWTFSSMTWTFS

they have been on a mission to chuck
out the chintz, but with the utmost
respect for original features

'Burransleh?' Mr Smith exclaimed with a puzzled look and a feeble Yorkshire accent. 'You said we were only going up the road.' I soothe his confused brow. 'Yes, dear, we're going to Barnsley in Gloucestershire. Now, get your wallet; we're in for a treat. This is meant to be one of the most stylish country-house hotels of them all.'

True, Barnsley is only an hour and a bit from London, but it's blissfully free of noise, streetlights, stress and strain. Barnsley House itself is an imposing grade II-listed manor-house within 11 acres of grounds, designed by former owner Rosemary Verey, the legendary gardener, designer and writer.

When we check in, the paint is scarcely dry but, considering what a new-born project this is, we sense none of the usual teething problems. The atmosphere is distinctly chilled. Our enthusiasm grows when we see the wall-mounted flat-screen TV. And the bottle of complimentary champagne (also distinctly chilled) that arrives within minutes doesn't go down too badly, either.

Now, I have a bit of a thing for bathrooms. And, quite frankly, this is a bathroom with an ensuite bedroom. The showerhead's the size of a dinner plate, and there's a double-ended rolltop bath; so, no arguments about who gets the tap end. (I suppose you could bicker about who gets to lie facing the second wall-mounted plasma-screen TV, but that would just be silly).

The ultra-cool modern furniture doesn't seem remotely out of place in 17th-century Barnsley House. Owners Tim and Rupert have certainly been on a mission to chuck out the chintz, but they have done so with the utmost respect for original features. The reception desk consists of a piece of glass mounted on a rough chunk of local stone – a detail that epitomises the whole vibe of the place. Old and new are blended effortlessly together here. The muted tones of the traditional paints make a perfect backdrop to the B&B Italia square-backed swivel armchairs. In the lounge, you may well find yourself flicking through an antique edition of *The Pickwick Papers* by the light of a funky chrome table lamp.

Tim and Rupert also own the pub, so you can charge everything to your room. Dangerous, I know, but should your tab detain you past daylight hours, there is a Maglite attached to each room

key. For lunch I opt for grilled lemon sole with gnocchi and roasted vegetables; my health-freak 'carbs are evil' boyfriend has his protein fix in the form of roast pork loin with lentils and aioli. The service is impeccable, the food is delicious, and Dr Atkins wouldn't be offended. Well, not until we order the warm ginger cake with toffee sauce and condensed-milk ice-cream, anyway.

The ensuing sugar rush propels us into Rosemary Verey's award-winning garden to see what all the fuss is about. Visitors used to flock from all around the world to see her work but, these days, the gardens are reserved for the exclusive pleasure of the hotel guests. We're like a couple of kids let loose in a playground – playing on the swing, taking to the lawns on an old pair of wooden stilts, and foraging in bushes to find secret dens. Whether or not you're into gardens, this one will blow you away; the best bit is the kitchen garden, which is

loaded with every kind of organic vegetable (don't be surprised if that bit of rocket you're eyeing up turns up on your plate later on).

Siesta time back at Room 3 is a whole new realm of pleasure: a seven-foot bed with cool, crisp Egyptian cotton sheets; luxurious feather duvet; fresh lilies from the garden; a panel of brushed-chrome dimmer switches at the bedside to vary the room's lighting; cable TV; remote-controlled CD and DVD...

In the stylish hotel restaurant we dine on delicious regional Italian cuisine. Consulting chef Franco Taruschio bases his menu around what they dig up for him in the veg patch that day. If you choose, you can dine alfresco under heaters in either the Gothic Summer House or the Temple, overlooking the lily pond. This is one of the most romantic hotels we have ever stayed at. The house is perfectly positioned for sunrise and sunset, and the whole garden is kitted out with lighting that changes with the night sky. It really is a slice of pure Gloucestershire heaven.

Reviewed by Stephanie Dennis

Need to know

Rooms 10.

Rates £270–£475.

Check-out Midday (5pm check-out with £75 supplement).

Facilities Tennis court, helicopter pad.

Kids The chef can prepare a child's meal at 6pm.

Also Considerate smoking permitted. There is a cigar bar in the basement.

In the know

Recommended rooms Room 1 has two baths in the bathroom, Room 2 has a Jacuzzi, Room 5 and 8 have a sitting room, and Room 7 its own conservatory and garden.

Packing tips Bubble-bath, CDs, tennis kit.

Food & drink

In the hotel Modern European, with home-grown vegetables.

Dress code Relaxed but stylish.

Top table Table 4, in the bay window.

Last orders Food: 9.30pm Monday–Thursday; 10pm Friday and Saturday. Bar opens late for guests.

Room service Food available in rooms while kitchen open.

Breakfast 7am–11am.

Local restaurants With two Michelin stars, **Le Champignon Sauvage** (01242 573449) serves English and French cuisine, and the **Daffodil** (01242 700055) serves Modern Mediterranean in an art deco room, both in Cheltenham.

Local bars Lively **Montpellier Wine Bar** in Cheltenham (01242 527774).

Local pubs The **Village Pub** (01285 740421) is an award-winning pub across the road. The **Trouble House Inn** in Tetbury (01666 502206) for exceptional-quality pub food. The **Bell** at Sapperton near Cirencester (01285 760298) for lunch and a great variety of ales.

Worth getting out of bed for

Have a picnic and watch a game at Cirencester Park Polo Club (01285 653225; www.cirencesterpolo.co.uk) or Beaufort Polo Club, favoured by the Prince of Wales and his sons (01666 880510; www.beaufortpoloclub.co.uk). Horse-riding and fishing can be organised by the hotel. Ballooning at Balloon Flights, Cheltenham (01242 675003; www.hot-air-ballooning.ltd.uk). Clay-pigeon shooting at Chatcombe Estate Shooting School (01242 870391). A walk through Coln Valley, just ten minutes away by car.

Diary March: Cheltenham Festival kicks off Britain's horse-racing calendar, and hosts the Gold Cup (01242 537642; www.cheltenham.co.uk). April/May: Badminton Horse Trials (01454 218272; www. badminton-horse.co.uk). August: Gatcombe Horse Trials at Gatcombe Park (www.gatcombe-horse.co.uk).

Smith A free Barnsley House champagne cocktail for each night of your stay.

Get a room! Check availability and make reservations through www.mrandmrssmith.com.

Barnsley House Barnsley House, Barnsley, Cirencester, Gloucestershire (01285 740000) info@barnsleyhouse.com; www.barnsleyhouse.com

Blakes

the rooms are the kind you
never want to leave

S S M T W T F ● M T W T F S S M T W T F S S M T W T

Style Seductive, stylish
Setting Secluded SW7

South Kensington

Blakes – the very name conjures up a whole era of modern decadence. The first time I visited Anouska Hempel's South Ken boutique hotel, it was to interview a famous film director who had decided to take a suite, with his glamorous girlfriend, for the filming of his new movie. The shoot ended up dragging on, unsurprisingly, for more than six months. I remember thinking what an indulgent gesture this was, but how he couldn't have bettered his choice. From the moment you walk up the steps into reception (the subtle oriental decor sets the tone for the whole hotel), Blakes whispers seductively: prepare to be seriously spoiled.

Arriving for a weekend with my boyfriend, I tried not to dwell on the enticing scenario of a six-month check-in. The receptionist barely missed a beat when we owned up to a complete lack of luggage; he kept formalities to a minimum, handed over a reassuringly old-fashioned, clunky room key, and led us through a rabbit warren of corridors and stairways to our suite. Simply put, the rooms at Blakes are the kind you never want to leave. Each has its own style, but all are inspired by various far-off lands: Russia, India, Turkey... The decor, while perhaps a little too redolent of the Eighties for some, is testament to Ms Hempel's impeccable taste and astonishing attention to detail. You realise very quickly

how Blakes earned its crown as the sexiest place in London to spend your wedding night (Patsy and Liam are just two of the hotel's high-profile honeymooners).

Our room, in short, screamed hedonism. For a start, the walls were black: a colour guaranteed to conjure up a James Bond feel (there is actually a suite in the hotel called the 007). And then, there was the bed. What a bed. Four-postered, festooned with burnt-orange and black drapes, and set provocatively in its own darkened niche, it oozed sex appeal all on its own. The bathroom was equally lavish, a homage to black and gilt, complete with oriental-style blinds. So cocoon-like was the whole setting that we were never quite sure what time of day it was – what more can you ask from a naughty weekend away?

There are 52 rooms at Blakes, though the super-swift service and discreet atmosphere allow you to feel as though you are the only people staying there. With a visit to the dining room, on the lower-ground floor, we saw for ourselves that there were some other guests, not to mention chic diners from the outside world. Bamboo, walls of black mirror-glass and dramatic spotlighting set a rather theatrical scene for what was a delicious supper. The menu, as one might expect, has a strong Eastern influence, but there are Western dishes, too. We opted for the Blakes blinis with caviar, and flirted with the excellent wine list before settling for a bottle of champagne. My one reservation is that women are still given an unpriced menu, which seems slightly out of touch, and could make the experience seem sleazy rather than romantic. The corner

tables are intimate, but others are better placed for people-watching opportunities. The staircase down to the restaurant is a definite focal point; try as you may to concentrate on your food or, indeed, your date, it's impossible not to wonder just who those slim Jimmy Choo-clad ankles could belong to. The dining room is also open for breakfast, but I advise the 'in bed' option. Nowhere have I tasted fresher orange juice or more expertly cooked scrambled eggs.

For those who can muster up the strength to escape from Blakes' opulent clutches, there is plenty to do. The retail extravaganza of Oxford, Regent and Bond Streets is a 20-minute cab ride away, but the more villagey area closer to hand gives you more flash for your cash. Brompton Cross, where Chanel, Ralph Lauren, Joseph, Paul Smith and other designer boutiques cluster around restaurants such as Daphne's and Bibendum, is a 10-minute walk away, and Harrods and Harvey Nichols are just beyond that. We decided to go for a stroll in Kensington Gardens, and popped in to see the exhibition at the Serpentine Gallery, where there are free must-see shows all year round.

There is no lavish spa here, nor any business facilities of note but then, being healthy and businesslike just isn't the point of a hotel like Blakes. If you want to feel like a film star for a weekend, though, or like a Bond girl/007 himself, then Blakes, with its superb suites and serious service, is the place for you. If there were ever a hotel for a lost weekend, then this, most definitely, is it.

Need to know

Rooms 50.

Rates £170–£1,295 (plus VAT).

Check-out Midday, but flexible.

Facilities Massage and therapy room with a full range of treatments (book in advance) and gym.

Kids Children very welcome; babysitters and nannies available on request.

In the know

Recommended rooms The Corfu Suite, which you enter from the garden; the Cardinal Suite (in luscious reds); the Empress Josephine Suite with tented bed and ebony-and-gold colour scheme; the library suite.

Packing tips Nothing practical.

Also Book restaurants well in advance.

Food & drink

In the hotel Modern European dining with Eastern influences.

Dress code Sheer glamour.

Top table Table 11, tucked away at the back of the restaurant. That said, all tables are good.

Last orders 10.45pm in the restaurant. You can order from room-service menu and eat in the Chinese Room (also known as Opium Den) 24 hours a day.

Room service 24 hours.

Breakfast 7am until late.

Local restaurants **Zuma** (020 7584 1010) for outstanding Japanese. **Mao Tai** (020 7731 2520) for mouthwatering Chinese in a contemporary setting. **San Lorenzo** (020 7584 1074) for Italian in Knightsbridge. A cab ride over the river takes you to **Chez Bruce** (020 8672 0114) for fine dining, and **Ransome's Dock** (020 7223 1611) for Modern European. Both have outstanding wine lists.

Local bars The **Collection** restaurant (020 7225 1212) for expert cocktails. **Bardot** (020 7351 1711), a small but perfectly formed designer bar. **K-Bar** (020 7352 6200) for drinks and dancing in Chelsea.

Local pubs The **Ifield** (020 7351 4900), a stylish pub with good food. The **Chelsea Ram** (020 7351 4008) for a lazy Sunday lunch. **Cooper's Arms** (020 7376 3120) for a pie and a pint.

Also The legendary **Kebab Kid** for a midnight feast on the New King's Road. And for an afternoon tea of thinly cut sandwiches, scones, jam and clotted cream, why not visit the **Ritz** (www.theritzhotel.co.uk/tea)?

Worth getting out of bed for

The Royal Albert Hall (020 7589 8212; www.royalalberthall.com). Shopping in Chelsea and Knightsbridge. UGC Fulham Cinema, a two-minute walk away. Kensington Palace. Serpentine Gallery in Kensington Gardens (020 7402 6075; www.serpentinegallery.org) holds free exhibitions.

Diary January: London International Boat Show (01784 473377; www.londonboatshow.net). May: Chelsea Flower Show (020 7649 1885; www.rhs.org.uk/chelsea). June: Wimbledon (020 8944 1066; www.wimbledon.org). July: the Proms, Royal Albert Hall. November: Christmas lights get switched on.

 A free bottle of champagne if booking a Luxury Double or Director Double; if booking a suite, a £50 voucher, to be redeemed against dinner for two in the restaurant.

Get a room! Check availability and make reservations through www.mrandmrssmith.com.

Blakes Hotel 33 Roland Gardens, London SW7 (020 7370 6701)
blakes@blakeshotels.com; www.blakeshotels.com

Blanch House

Style Laidback hedonism by the sea
Setting Brighton townhouse

every room is different, so pick whichever one you
think will enhance your own personal brighton fantasy

Brighton

I pick up the convertible from a friend, with the promise of a sunny drive down to the south coast with my lovely new girlfriend. As we speed down the M20, the clouds seem determined to hide the sunshine we'd hoped for, and the roof stays firmly over our heads. But with a night in Blanch House ahead of us, the weather does little to dampen our expectations.

Weaving our way through the Lanes, we eventually find the narrow street down to the seafront that we've been looking for (my sense of direction is about as good as my meteorological predictions). Finding no parking, I offload my new Mrs Smith with the bags outside what we think is Blanch House and cross my fingers that I can navigate my way back. When I do, my initial thoughts are: nice townhouse – wonder if anyone's in? Having rung the bell and telephoned several times, just as we're looking for pebbles to throw at the window, a man

arrives at the door. 'Sorry, I was on the phone,' he pants, 'and there's no one else here'. This leaves us in no doubt: this is one very laidback place. Just how we like it.

Having registered, we take our bags upstairs – I certainly didn't expect the poor man to double as a porter. As every room is different, you can pick whichever one you think will best enhance your own personal Brighton fantasy – we've chosen the Perrier Jouët suite. We open the door, and the decadence, the lush furnishings and the acres of bed inside damn near take our breath away. Green velvet curtains surrounding the room and a free-standing bath in the middle make it very, very sexy. It seems only right that we order a celebratory drink befitting our surroundings. We request an off-menu champagne cocktail – raspberry purée, Chambord, Stoli and, of course, Perrier Jouët – and it's a triumph.

The hotel's restaurant has a fantastic reputation so we'd thought to book ahead. It being a Thursday night, though, and since we ventured down a little late, it isn't overly busy and we are extremely well attended. Various herb-infused breads whet our appetites, along with a fruity bottle of Fleurie chosen from a wine list with plenty of favourites. The French-inspired dishes are delicious. Fed and watered, we are ready to find a little more mischief, and the receptionist suggests we take a short cab ride to the members' bar, the Ocean Rooms. After a cocktail in chic surrounds, we stroll down to the seafront, ending up at the Funky Buddha Lounge. Here, the cashier asks us for our NUS cards; considering I'm no longer eligible for an 18–30 holiday, this comes as a compliment. But a Seventies student night isn't quite the vibe we're after, so we retreat to our hotel bar.

very laid-back – just how we like it

Back in Blanch, we order a bottle of PJ (after all, I have to celebrate my new-found youth status) and cosy up on a banquette. Small and intimate, the bar is perfect for late-night fun, as previous guests like Damon Albarn, Gwyneth Paltrow and Noel Gallagher can no doubt testify. And, as anyone who has experienced irritating outbreaks of socialus interruptus at other hotels will be happy to hear, there are no schoolmarmish barmen tapping their watches. In fact, word has it the hotel owners are usually the last ones standing once the party has got going (as it tends to every weekend). In this particular instance, it's us.

The next morning, we're woken by the telephone. 'Just to remind you that your massage is booked for 10am.' Whoops. 'I'm afraid we ended up having rather a big night. Any chance we can stay a tiny bit longer?' Much laughter is followed by a 'no problem'. After grabbing a little more sleep, and some breakfast in bed, we eventually check out at about 1.30pm, having paid a mere tenner for the privilege. By now, the sun has even appeared, and a hair of the dog on Brighton's seafront is beckoning.

Reviewed by Ben Sowton

Need to know

Rooms 12: four Queens, five Kings and three suites.
Rates £125–£220, including breakfast; £125–£220 at the weekend.
Check-out 11am or later if the room isn't booked (£10 supplement).
Facilities In-room massages by arrangement.
Kids Very welcome, although partying can get a little hectic and, therefore, noisy at the weekends. Pet-friendly, too.

In the know

Recommended rooms The Perrier Jouët suite, luxurious in green velvet.
The White Suite, with Jacuzzi. The Decadence Suite, with free-standing bath.
Packing tips Marabou mules; jelly shoes.
Also No private parking. Minimum two-night stay at weekends.

Food & drink

In the hotel Contemporary Brit-with-a-twist cuisine. Closed Sundays and Mondays.
Dress code Most guests dress up.
Top table They are all good.
Last orders Food: 10pm. Bar: open to non-residents until 11; to guests, until 12, or 4ish at the weekend.
Room service None as such.
Breakfast 9.30am–11am at weekends; 9am–10.30am in the week.
Local restaurants **Havana** (01273 773388) is a Cuban-inspired contemporary eatery and bar. **Quod** (01273 202070) is a bar and restaurant serving Italian-inspired food. The **Saint** (01273 607835) serves up Modern British food. The **Regency** (01273 325014) and **English's** (01273 327980) are traditional fish places.
Local bars **Koba** (01273 720059) is an intimate cocktail bar, but we prefer **Heist** on West Street (01273 822555). **Funky Buddha Lounge** (01273 733371) and the three-floored **Ocean Rooms** (01273 699069) are open late.
Local pubs The **Sidewinder** is almost next door, and so good you might get no further.
Setting Sun (01273 626192) has amazing views and does a great Sunday lunch.

Worth getting out of bed for

The Duke of York's independent cinema (www.dukeofyorkscinema.com). Water sports at Hove Lagoon or Brighton Marina (www.hovelagoon.co.uk). Kayaks for hire on the beachfront, under the arches near the Zap club.
Diary May: Brighton Festival is like a south-coast Edinburgh Fringe (www.brighton-festival.org.uk). November: paganistic thrills on bonfire night in Lewes.

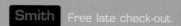 Free late check-out.

Get a room! Check availability and make reservations through www.mrandmrssmith.com.

Blanch House 17 Atlingworth Street, Brighton (01273 603504)
info@blanchhouse.co.uk; www.blanchhouse.co.uk

Burgh Island Hotel

MTWTFSSMTWTF MTWTFSSMTWTFSSMTWTFSSMTW

Style Art deco splendour
Setting English Channel idyll

back to the golden era of british deco when chrome and plastic mixed with machine-age motifs

Bigbury-on-Sea

S S M T W T F S S M T W T F S S M T W T F S

BURGH ISLAND

'Welcome to Burgh Island, 007. We have been expecting you. Your code is 5814. Your driver will be with you shortly.' Was it my imagination, or did the voice on the line just call me 007? Following written instructions, we had called reception from the red telephone box (no mobile signal here) in the hamlet of St Anne's Chapel, two miles from our destination. The code I was given would allow us to enter a gated car enclosure; our driver was to be Trevor, replete with Land-Rover Defender, a moustache that seemed to have grown bigger every time I looked at him, and the look of a man who had seen it all before.

We, on the other hand, had never seen anything like this before. As we descended into Bigbury-on-Sea and saw the remarkable art deco hotel that dominates the island, we had a hunch that the adventure had only just begun. Separated from the rugged Devon coastline by a natural sand causeway some 200 metres long, Burgh Island is revered by locals and visitors alike – and for good reason.

Built in 1929 as a playground for 'Uncle Archie' Nettlefold and friends, the ocean-liner styled country house opened as a hotel in 1932; Winston Churchill, Noël Coward and Agatha Christie were all guests during its post-war heyday. Glancing at Trevor's in-car satellite-navigation system as he drove us across the beach, however, I still felt it was rather more Ian Fleming than Agatha Christie. (Perhaps if it had been high tide and we had taken the four-metre-tall sea tractor instead of the Defender, I might not have felt so much like an international man of mystery.)

Entering the hotel, you are transported 70 years back in time to the golden era of British deco, when chrome and plastic mixed elegantly with mirrors and machine-age motifs. Big-band jazz crackles out from Bose speakers, and sophisticated guests sip dry martinis in the Palm Court lounge, as sharply dressed porters whisk away your luggage. I felt certain Hercule Poirot was on the premises. Perhaps he could help me solve the mystery of Trevor the tractor driver's burgeoning moustache?

We had booked the Garden Suite, the largest of the 21 bedrooms. The word 'large' can't begin to describe it: with vast bedroom, titanic lounge and two bathrooms, if it were an apartment in Notting Hill, it would be worth more than the whole island. Everything in the hotel is historically accurate. Even the classic Bush radio was pre-tuned to a station playing Thirties jazz. Though everything is superbly comfortable, we weren't expecting modern perfection. As Burgh Island's website had told us, many of the pieces are old, if not original to the hotel. The ultimate draw of this flagship room is its floor-to-ceiling French windows, which provide a spectacular view of the Devonshire coastline and open onto a grassy garden where, in warm weather, you can partake of your own private dining experience.

Having decided that Monsieur Poirot must be having a day off from mystery-solving, we decided to explore the island, which includes a helicopter pad, tennis courts, and a natural seawater swimming pool at the base of the cliffs. Nine minutes later, we were sitting snugly in the Pilchard Inn (est. 1336), watching the tide begin to swallow the beach below. As Steve the landlord told us about the resident smuggler's ghost, the two seas slowly covered the causeway and the island's only link to the mainland disappeared. You could just picture summer swimmers scrambling for their

lilos, uncertain if they'll make it back to shore in time. We heard how, at very high tides, when it's blowing a gale, not even Trevor's tractor can make it across, and both staff and guests are stranded until the waters part once more.

We had received quite specific instructions about dinner, which explained that black tie and 'proper' evening dresses are quite normal. We were amazed to see that nearly all the women were in eveningwear, and more than half the men were doing their best to imitate Pierce Brosnan. Set against such a background of grandeur and spectacle, the food might easily have been secondary but, in true Burgh Island style, it was perfect, down to the last detail. The clean, modern cuisine was surpassed only by the seamless service, and an atmosphere that carried you back to a time of ocean liners, skyscrapers and cocktails.

Burgh Island is a place like no other. It's a destination hotel, where people go to get married; to celebrate an anniversary; or just to lose themselves for a weekend. You don't need to be James Bond or Hercule Poirot to stay there, but you do need to be prepared to have an unforgettable adventure. And, as for Trevor's burgeoning facial hair, it was Agatha Christie who once wrote: 'The gentleman with the large moustache seems most agreeable.' There you are – mystery solved.

Need to know

Rooms 23, mostly suites with balcony and sea view.

Rates £275–£425, including breakfast and dinner.

Check-out 11.30am.

Facilities Dedicated masseuse and acupuncturist, tennis courts, billiards, sauna, natural seawater pool, helipad, access to gym and pool on the mainland.

Kids Special children's menu and high tea in the Kid's Den; no children under three.

Also Smoking only permitted in the bar.

In the know

Recommended rooms The Artist's Studio, also known as Captain Hornblower's Retirement Lovenest. For pure deco, ask for Noël Coward (where private dining is available) or Avon. The biggest suite is the Garden Suite.

Packing tips Beachwear and formal attire.

Also The island has one pub, the Pilchard Inn.

Food & drink

In the hotel The Ganges Room serves breakfast and lunch (on the terrace, weather permitting). The Pilchard Inn does delicious pub fare with a seafood slant. The grand, elegant art deco ballroom also specialises in fish.

Dress code Formal elegance.

Top table Ask for a sea view.

Last orders Lunch: 2pm. Dinner: 8.45pm. Bar: 2am.

Room service Until 2am, within reason.

Breakfast 8.30am–10am.

Local restaurants Matisse Restaurant (01548 831100) in Ermington, near Plymouth, does fresh fish and seafoods caught off West Country beaches, with fantastic views. Restaurant 42 (01548 843408) serves Modern European in stylish surrounds.

Local pubs The Sloop Inn in Bantham (01548 560489) is renowned for its fine local meat and delicious puddings. The Fortescue Inn in Salcombe (01548 842868) is popular for its fish. The Ship Inn in Noss Mayo (01752 872387) is a waterside pub for a steak and a pint.

Worth getting out of bed for

Tennis, boules, dolphin-watching, a stroll along the beach followed by cocktails on the terrace. Swimming in the natural rock pool. Diving at Diventure Salcombe (01548 843663), which caters for all levels of experience. For sailing, try Dinghy Sailing (01548 842786; www.salcombedinghysailing. co.uk). For helicopter trips, contact AH Helicopter Services (01647 277533).

Diary Balls throughout the year, including the Valentine's Ball in February, the Summer Ball in July and the Hallowe'en Ball in October. July: World Offshore Powerboat Championships, Plymouth (www.c1ukpowerboat.com).

Smith Complimentary cocktails during film screenings.

Get a room! Check availability and make reservations through www.mrandmrssmith.com.

Burgh Island Hotel Burgh Island, Bigbury-on-Sea, South Devon (01548 810514) reception@burghisland.com; www.burghisland.com

Charlton House

M T W T F ▇ M T W T F S S M T W T F S S M T W T F S S M T

Style Mulberry cordial
Setting Rolling West Country

somewhere between the grand austerity of
old-style country retreat and in-vogue homely chic

Shepton Mallet

FSSMTWTFSSMTWTFSSMTWTFSSMTWTFSS

The motorway, Friday. Rush hour. To cut a familiar story short (unlike our trek), our planned three-hour journey to Charlton House ended up taking seven. To say we were tired and stressed by the time we got there would be a classic of understatement, though the mood did begin to lift once we found ourselves moving through the undulating Somerset countryside. And we found it first time, just outside Shepton Mallet: the classic manor-house, with an Italianate stone fountain in its serenely beautiful courtyard. Things were definitely looking up.

A charming young man, all rosy cheeks and round spectacles, helped us to our room, a standard double called Strawberry Hill (all the rooms here are individually decorated, and named accordingly) in the Lodge, which is annexed to the main house. These rooms are a little smaller than the suites and deluxe offerings next door, but you get your own private courtyard by way of recompense. All the rooms are

sumptuous in feel, owing mainly to the fact that Charlton House is owned by Roger and Monty Saul, founders of luxury-goods label Mulberry. The hotel doubles as a showcase for its designs, and the quality of the furnishings and fabrics – mixed and matched throughout – is as high as you'd expect. Radical or minimalist this is not; instead, Charlton House occupies a happy middle ground, somewhere between the grand austerity of the old-style country retreat and an in-vogue homely chic.

Mulberry items are everywhere you look. We particularly liked touches such as the vintage Roberts radio, the Congo leather wallet containing guest information, and the Mulberry teddy bear waiting on our bed to greet us. All these products are, of course, available to buy in reception; and the hotel already has your credit-card number, should you decide to accidentally pack any of them. No prizes, then, for guessing the name of the restaurant... The Mulberry restaurant is Charlton House's other big selling point: a Michelin-starred kitchen, where chef Adam Fellows produces creative dishes using the finest locally sourced ingredients.

We found the staff charming, with that wonderful French ability to make you feel like a million dollars: where every choice you make from the menu is the best one, and the mid-price wine you pick is the bargain of the century. There wasn't even any smirking when Mrs Smith lost her place on the wine list and asked for 'the German white, the one from the Rhone valley'. Three courses were included in our £240-a-night room rate, though you can pay a supplement and go for a more expensive seven-course menu gourmand, which we thought we'd try on our second night.

Our bed, with proper goose-feather pillows and a sensuous velvet bedspread, gave us a wonderful night's sleep, and we woke in the morning feeling ready for anything. Our good friend on reception had furnished us with leaflets promoting a variety of local attractions: Cheddar Gorge was rejected by the girlfriend on the grounds that she's allergic to cheese; I don't know what Wookey Hole is, exactly, but it sounded too much like a pornographic version of *Star Wars*. Glastonbury is just down the road, but this wasn't festival season and, in any case, it was raining heavily. Instead, we took the in-car option of the safari park at nearby Longleat House, which has most of the animal kingdom's bases covered: giraffes, water buffalo, monkeys, rhinos, antelopes, deer, tigers, wolves and, of course, the famous lions of Longleat. It's really rather brilliant, especially if you can work yourself up into a childlike state of expectation. Mrs Smith found my 'throwing her to the wolves/lions' joke hilarious the first couple of times.

There must be countless decent country pubs in the area around Charlton House but we forgot to ask our man at reception, and ended up in front of a big screen watching the football in a pub in Shepton Mallet itself. There was a good atmosphere in terms of football chants but I wouldn't really

recommend it – not unless the Slaughtered Lamb scene from *An American Werewolf in London* is your idea of a good night out.

It was back to the Mulberry Restaurant for dinner, which was a complete treat. The only distraction from the saddle of rabbit and seared John Dory came from two men at a nearby table; we strained to hear their conversation, trying to work out just who were the dark-haired actor and film director sitting there. We never found out. Charlton House is far too discreet for that. Feeling refreshed and relaxed, we did, however, come to the conclusion that life as Mr and Mrs Mulberry among velvety drapes and oriental rugs would suit us just fine.

Reviewed by Matt Turner

Need to know

Rooms 25, each individually decorated with Mulberry fabrics.

Rates £165–£425, including breakfast and newspaper.

Check-out 11am.

Facilities As well as treatments, Monty's Spa has indoor and outdoor pools, steam room, sauna, experience showers, laconium, wet treatment room, tennis court and gym; golf can be arranged.

Kids Welcome. An agency provides nannies and babysitting.

Also No smoking in the restaurant, but permitted in one lounge and six of the bedrooms. The Mulberry factory shop offers the widest range outside Bond Street, at reduced prices.

In the know

Recommended rooms The Secret Garden Room and wood-pannelled Chesterblade for the terrace and garden view; Ostler with its free-standing copper bath; South Wing for its giant four-poster. Generally, rooms overlooking the gardens at the back have the best view.

Packing tips Leave room to take some Mulberry home with you.

Food & drink

In the hotel Traditional meets exotic in the Michelin-starred restaurant; private dining available.

Dress code Think *Brideshead Revisited*.

Top table Perhaps go for a seat around the edge; in summer, the conservatory is lovely.

Last orders Food: 9.30pm. Bar: open all night.

Room service 24 hours.

Breakfast 7.30am–10am; 8am–10am on Sundays.

Local restaurants The **Thatched Cottage Inn** across the road (01749 342058) suits all palates. **The Moody Goose** at The Old Priory (01761 416784. **Blostin's Restaurant** (01749 343648) offers Anglo-French cuisine (closed Sundays and Mondays).

Local pubs A 15th-century coaching house, the **Talbot Inn** (01373 812254) serves fresh fish and game in season. The **Three Horseshoes** in Batcombe (01749 850359) is a traditional English pub with open fires. The **Strode Arms** at Cranmore (01749 880450) has exceptional well-presented food.

Worth getting out of bed for

The hotel can organise horse-riding. Cheddar Gorge is touristy but also an area of outstanding beauty (www.cheddarcaves.co.uk). Wells is six miles away and Bath 19 miles away. Longleat (www.longleat.co.uk) has numerous attractions including the house, a safari park, a maze, a railway and more. Glastonbury Abbey (www.glastonburyabbey.com). Trout fishing at Temple Cloud (01761 452423). Golfing at the Isle of Wedmore (www.wedmoregolfclub.com).

Diary May: Bath International Music Festival (01225 463362; www.bathmusicfest.org.uk). August: Glastonbury Classical Festival offers the more sedate side of the musical spectrum (01458 832020, www.glastonburyfestivals.co.uk/classical); International Balloon Festival, Bristol (0117 953 5884; www.bristolfiesta.co.uk) – mass hot-air-balloon launches.

Smith A free bottle of champagne on arrival and ten per cent off massage and beauty treatments.

Get a room! Check availability and make reservations through www.mrandmrssmith.com.

Charlton House Shepton Mallet, near Bath, Somerset (01749 342008)
enquiry@charltonhouse.com; www.charltonhouse.com

Style State-of-the-art comfort
Setting Charming Chipping Campden

The Cotswold House Hotel

Chipping Campden

each room is different and has its own USP

As you climb into your car on a Friday night and negotiate the inevitable fume-filled crawl out of town, you always experience a little tremor up your spine, I find. Firstly, because you're leaving the filthy, dirty, sordid city behind you for something fresh, natural and healthy, and secondly because you're thinking: 'Oh my God, how the hell am I going to cope without a skinny latté, freshly cut sushi and 24-hour I-want-I-get urban living?' Then you quit the motorway, and the little B-roads that twist through chocolate-box villages remind you that you are on an adventure and really the country is quite sweet, and perhaps you should steel yourself and be brave. Well, at the Cotswold House Hotel you have

absolutely nothing to fear. If you suddenly feel a long way from your widescreen TV and Philippe Starck power shower, relax. Cotswold House is your dream designer pad, in a breathtaking rural setting.

Now – a word about dirty weekends: whoever you're with, the destination *has* to justify the journey. If you're taking your long-term partner, you're probably after a little 'you time', or your sex life needs a pep-up. In either case, a dodgy bed, musty wardrobe and nylon bedspread just won't cut it. If you are going away with a new love, though your passion might dictate you'd have a good time if you were camping in a field in the rain, you probably don't know each other that well, and everything you do and say creates an impression. And do you want to create a second-hand, tight-arsed, bed-and-breakfast image, or one of effortless cool and

sophistication? Hmm, that's a toughie. If you are taking the man/girl of your dreams away for a weekend, then you just can't afford to take any chances. To justify a schlep away from the comfort of home, you'd better make sure the end result is spot-on. And if that means luxury, security and the softest pillows money can buy, then the Cotswold House Hotel is the one for you.

Chipping Campden is the stuff that tourist-board dreams are made of – ancient, higgledy-piggledy low-lying buildings of beautiful yellow Cotswold stone. When we visited, the whole place was doused in cherry blossom; Hallmark couldn't have done it better. Here, in the midst of several B&Bs, two newsagents, four antique shops, six pubs and precious little else, Cotswold House stands proud. Its 17th-century façade and warm glowing windows defy you not to be tempted inside. Soft, squishy furniture, a crackling log fire and super-friendly (but not unctuous) staff immediately put you at ease before you're whisked off to your room upstairs, or across the courtyard to one of the cottages.

Each room is different from the next and has its own USP – aubergine satin bedding (too, too luxurious), sloping attic ceilings, four-poster bed or awesome bathing palace (you can choose from the pictures on the website, so there are no shocks when you get there). Each room comes equipped with a massive television, Bang & Olufsen entertainment centre, one of the biggest and comfiest beds you will ever have the joy of sleeping in and – yup – Philippe Starck in the bathrooms.

Embarrassingly, this reviewer and her Mr Smith saw little reason to move from said bed, and spent the bulk of the weekend with champagne in hand watching several of the hotel's large collection of DVDs, and doing all those things that

Mr and Mrs Smiths are meant to do. However, on Saturday we had gorgeous elevenses in the hotel's charming walled garden, underneath the apple blossom, and happily allowed coffee to segue into pre-lunch rosé. The hotel's main restaurant doesn't open until evening, but Caesar salad from the all-day brasserie did the trick. The charm of Chipping Campden managed, in the end, to lure us out, and we embarked on a walk to Pilkington through the fields. In the event, though, it seemed a long, long way to go, so we abandoned the fields and hedgerows in favour of the safety and comfort of Cotswold House, not to mention the lure of fine dining courtesy of chef Jamie Forman. After all, a dirty weekend is one thing, but a muddy afternoon is quite another.

Reviewed by Tiffanie Darke

Need to know

Rooms 30.
Rates £130–£650, including breakfast.
Check-out Midday.
Facilities DVD and CD library.
Kids There is a children's menu, and cots and high chairs. Fold-away beds provided for £35.
Also Smoking not permitted in the Garden Restaurant. Dogs and cats can be accommodated.

In the know

Recommended rooms The Grammar School Suite has two bedrooms, two bathrooms and a kitchen. Four suites have private gardens, including two with hot tubs. Rooms 17 and 25 have the best view. The new rooms in Montrose House include bathrooms with huge limestone baths; try and get the one with the steam room for two.
Packing tips Something more comfortable to slip into.
Also Pre-order your minibar so it stocks what you want, specify how you'd like the bed made up (feather pillows, etc) and request the toiletries you'd like.

Food & drink

In the hotel Juliana's Restaurant serves Modern British/Continental cuisine. Hick's Brasserie for informal, café-style eating; in fair weather have coffee or snacks on the Pavilion Terrace.
Dress code No jeans or trainers in the Garden Restaurant.
Top table Dine outside, weather permitting; inside, near the French windows.
Last orders Food: 9.30pm in both restaurants. Bar: as late as residents like.
Room service Kitchen closes at 9.30pm; anything else, up to midnight.
Breakfast 8am–11.30am.
Local restaurants Le Champignon Sauvage (01242 573449) and the Bacchanalian Restaurant (01242 227713) offer fine-dining experiences in Cheltenham. Oriental fusion menu at The Noel Arms Hotel (01386 840317); for gastro fare, duck into Dover's Bar.
Local bars Montpellier Wine Bar in Cheltenham (01242 527774) has a lively atmosphere.
Local pubs The Feathers at Woodstock (01993 812291) is a well-respected inn.

Worth getting out of bed for

Archery, quad-biking, hot-air ballooning and clay-pigeon shooting can be arranged through Rob Ireland (01608 650413). For horse-riding, try Jill Gabb (01386 584250) or Willersey Stables (01386 858189). Coarse fishing at the Lemington Lakes (01608 650872) or trout fishing at Salford Trout Lakes (01608 643209).
Diary March: Cheltenham races, including Gold Cup (www.cheltenham.co.uk); polo at Cirencester Park Polo Club (www.cirencesterpolo.co.uk). May–December: horse-racing at Stratford-upon-Avon (www.stratfordracecourse.net). June/July: Longborough Opera Festival (www.longboroughopera.com). October: Cheltenham Festival of Literature (www.cheltenhamfestivals.co.uk).

Smith Choose from afternoon tea for two, a bottle of Hermès scent, or a bottle of champagne.

Get a room! Check availability and make reservations through www.mrandmrssmith.com.

The Cotswold House Hotel The Square, Chipping Campden, Gloucestershire (01386 840330) reception@cotswoldhouse.com; www.cotswoldhouse.com

...strip poker

How to play

How to play strip poker (five-card draw)

Each player should make sure they are suitably well clad before the game begins; a roughly level playing field is only fair. The dealer shuffles up a complete deck of cards. Each player puts in the ante (see **poker betting**, below), and is dealt five cards face down. Next it's a clockwise round of betting. Each player then has the option to discard up to three cards and have them replaced with fresh cards from the top of the pack. There is another round of betting before the hands are revealed; the highest hand wins the pot (see below) and the lowest hand takes off an item of clothing before the game continues. The game continues in this fashion until one or all players are entirely naked, depending on the exact circumstances, and motives for playing in the first place…

Poker betting

A friendly game would usually have an ante of 5p, 10p or 20p. The money is put in the centre of the table and is called the pot. You have three choices when the betting gets to you: **Call** – betting enough to match what has been bet since the last time you bet, for example: if you bet 20p and somebody then bid 30p, you would owe 10p. If you call, you put that 10p into the pot and stay in the hand. **Raise** – let's say the initial bet is 20p: you'd match that, and then add the sum you wish to raise by. Now the other players will either call, raise, or fold. The round continues until everybody has called or folded on a bet. **Fold** – dropping out of the current hand: you only lose what you have put in the pot up to the point of folding.

And remember: you lose, you strip.

Poker hands

Straight flush A straight (five cards in order, such as 7-8-9-10-J), all of the same suit. Aces can be high or low. An ace-high straight flush is called a **Royal Flush** and is the highest natural hand.

Four of a kind Four cards of the same rank, eg: four aces or four kings. If two or more hands qualify, the hand with the highest-rank four wins.

Full house A full house is a three of a kind and a pair, such as K-K-K-2-2. When there are two full houses, the tie is broken by the higher-ranking three of a kind.

Flush A hand in which all the cards are the same suit, such as 5-7-9-J-Q, all of diamonds. When there are two or more flushes, the flush containing the highest card wins.

Straight Five cards in rank order, for example: A-2-3-4-5, but not of the same suit. Aces can be high or low. When there are two straights, the highest straight wins. If two straights have the same value, the pot is split.

Three of a kind Three cards of any rank, with the remaining cards not a pair. As with the full house, the highest-ranking three of a kind wins.

Two pair Two distinct pairs and a fifth card. The higher-ranking pair wins ties. If both hands have the same high pair, the second pair wins. If both hands have the same pairs, the high card (see below) wins.

Pair One pair, with three other cards. The highest-ranking pair wins. High card breaks ties.

High card When no player has even a pair, it comes down to who is holding the highest-ranking card. If there is a tie for the high card, the next high card determines the pot.

SSMTWTFSSMTWTFSSMTWTFSSMTWTF ■ MTWTFSSMT

Style London luxury
Setting West End world

Covent Garden Hotel

an excellent vantage point for
seeing all manner of london
life strut or crawl past

There's no feeling to match that of being slap bang in the heart of it all, with swinging London on your doorstep. The Covent Garden Hotel couldn't be better located for every kind of West End experience: galleries, shopping, theatre, clubbing – or just watching the world go by. It's a hop and a skip from the Seven Dials roundabout on Monmouth Street: an excellent vantage point for seeing all manner of London life strut or crawl past. Monmouth Street itself is on the edge of Covent Garden's main shopping area, and has some very enticing shops, such as CoCo de Mer, Kiehl's, I Love Voyage, Koh Samui and the Loft, just waiting to gobble your plastic.

Checking into a swanky hotel in the capital is always going to have a touch of the film star about it; the wonderful thing about this hotel is that while it certainly caters for the well-heeled and deep-pocketed, it also works hard at a genuinely laid-back, home-from-home atmosphere. The entrance has a smart and formal English appearance, softened by down-to-earth staff (the concierge, Nicky, is a trouper who can sort out anything, from umbrellas to show tickets). The decor of our bedroom is more traditional than the lobby areas: tapestry and paisley fabrics, and the CGH's signature dressmaker's models feature in all the rooms – very Establishment, and charming for it. We find the usual facilities, from an extensive minibar to VCR, with unexpected touches such as the quintessentially English Roberts radio next to the bed.

Once checked in, we set off for lunch 'all the way' over in Marylebone, wanting to check out the Orrery – apparently the jewel in Terence Conran's empire. It takes us barely half an hour to walk there; we Tube-dependent Londoners forget that so many areas are within walking distance of the centre – Hyde Park, Green Park, the Embankment. From Monmouth Street, you have the option of any number of outings, with the promise of a return, every time, to the calm sanctuary of the hotel (and the daily pick-me-up neck massage offered free to guests).

Before heading to the boudoir for a bath and a roll around on the very roomy bed, we drop by the sitting room for a G&T from the Honesty Bar. Mr Smith sorts out the drinks, and I sink into an armchair built for two to check out the company: foreign families, businessmen, fashionistas and media types – and, oh my goodness, it's an actor from Hollywood's A-list. I sidle up to Mr Smith as casually as I can and proudly whisper my celeb spot. We turn around slowly, looking at our shoes, the ceiling, in a vain attempt to conceal our true intent of celeb staring. Mr Smith sounds as though he's having an asthma attack, and turns me back the other way, gripping my arm frantically. 'No, it's Boromir.' I nod enthusiastically. Well, he has watched *Lord of the Rings* 16 times.

HONESTY BAR

Once washed and coiffed, we proceed to the 54-seater private cinema (complete with state-of-the-art THX technology and vast cream leather seats). Saturday night is Saturday Film Club, which combines a three-course dinner with the film of the week for the bargain price of £30 a head – the fun bit being you can arrange your dinner around the film: starter beforehand; main course and pudding as a chaser. It was certainly an intimate affair – just six of us watching *The Maltese Falcon*. We ate in the hotel's restaurant, Brasserie Max, which serves Modern British food in an airy art deco room.

Next we're off out and about the buzzing streets of Covent Garden and Soho. The Lab bar on Old Compton Street is a great place with hip folk sipping swish cocktails, right in the thick of it all. After veering into Bar Italia on Frith Street for a steadying latte stop, we headed back to the hotel, picking up the Sunday papers on the way. We head straight to the honesty bar and, topped up with double vodkas, emerge into the smaller of the two lounge areas. There's a party of eight celebrating an engagement: will we join them? Smiles all round – yes – and, again, a sharp intake of breath from Mr Smith. Another great celeb spot. Twenty minutes later, and I am singing my heart out solo to 'Streets of London' (no reason, it was just that time of night) as a famous comedy actress hushes the ensemble with cries of 'Go on, girl!'. That's another great thing about this place – you never know quite who you'll bump into next.

Reviewed by Mr & Mrs Smith

Need to know

Rooms 58.

Rates £195–£795 (plus VAT).

Check-out 11am.

Facilities Gym, beauty room (book treatments in advance), library, state-of-the-art cinema.

Kids Children welcome, babysitting and nannies available by prior arrangement.

Also Classic films screened on Saturdays at 8pm.

In the know

Recommended rooms The Loft Suite is where Armani's fashion entourage often stay.
The Four-poster Suite has a plasma screen and the largest bed in London, measuring eight foot square.

Packing tips Opera glasses.

Also Book restaurants and theatre tickets well in advance.

Food & drink

In the hotel Brasserie Max serves fabulous Modern European.

Dress code No jacket required.

Top table Ask for a table away from the entrance.

Last orders 11pm in both restaurant and bar.

Room service 24 hours.

Breakfast 7am–11am.

Local restaurants **BKB** in Soho (020 7734 5656) for inexpensive bistro food in buzzy surrounds. Eat up at the bar at **Le Caprice** (020 7629 2239): fantastic for people-watching. **Hakkasan** (020 7927 7000) for the best Modern Asian. Celebrity favourite the **Ivy** (020 7836 4751). **Locanda Locatelli** (020 7935 9088) for Michelin-starred Italian. The **Savoy Grill** (020 7592 1600) for the best in Modern British. See www.gordonramsay.com for details of Gordon Ramsay's outstanding London restaurants. Local clubs and bars **Chinawhite** (020 7343 0040) is louche and decadent. **CVO Firevault** (020 7580 5333) a cosy bar beneath a showroom. **Salvador & Amanda** (020 7240 1551) is a DJ bar with tapas. **Windows** at the Hilton (020 7493 8000) on the 28th floor. **Bar Italia** (020 7437 4520) serves espressos into the small hours. **Lab** (020 7437 7820) is a bar with mean mixologists. Local pubs The **Endurance** in Soho (020 7437 2944) for a pint or posh pub grub.

Worth getting out of bed for

All the West End theatres are on your doorstep (www.ticketmaster.co.uk), as is the Royal Opera House (www.royalopera.org). Major art spaces include the National Gallery (www.nationalgallery.org.uk) and Tate Modern (www.tate.org.uk). See the city from the London Eye (www.londoneye.com). Take a riverboat cruise from Embankment to Greenwich (www.londontown.com/sightseeing). Somerset House (www.somerset-house.org.uk) for ice-skating in the winter and concerts in the summer.

Diary June: Spitalfields Festival for classical music concerts (www.spitalfieldsfestival.org.uk).

September: London Open House weekend (www.londonopenhouse.org), when buildings of architectural and cultural interest open their doors to the public. November: London Film Festival (www.lff.org.uk).

Smith A complimentary bottle of house champagne on arrival.

Get a room! Check availability and make reservations through www.mrandmrssmith.com.

Covent Garden Hotel 10 Monmouth Street, London WC2 (020 7806 1000)
covent@firmdale.com; www.firmdale.com

Cowley Manor

Style Funked-up stately home
Setting Acres of spectacular Cotswolds

Cowley

minimal lines and block colours give it a swedish feel

Nothing can quite prepare you for Cowley Manor. Firstly, if you didn't know it was there, you could quite easily drive on by, none the wiser. And, second, once you have taken in the astonishing grandeur of the Italianate stone house, you may think yourself convinced that whatever is within cannot match it (just you wait). We were met on arrival by very lovely, very welcoming staff members in purple jumpers (I felt sorry for them sweltering away in wool, but I guess the 'uniform' is more in keeping with the Cowley ethos than full livery), and entered with an open mind.

The reception hallway is dominated by a spectacular crystal chandelier, composed of hundreds of prisms that catch the light: so far, little to indicate the stately's past life. I set off to explore, entering the connected bar and lounge area; these are large, high-ceilinged spaces, with a decor that comes as a complete shock to me. To call the look 'designer' doesn't do justice to Cowley's funky, flamboyant aesthetic; the effect of cowhide window seats, red laminate tables and comical papier-mâché 'hunting trophies' is certainly a world away from the usual country-house hotels. It was, however, clever to leave the dining room

intact to give guests a hint of the house's former glory: the floor-to-ceiling wood panelling is all original, the views of the gardens are wonderful, and the sheer scale of the room is extremely impressive. Giant, modern cone-shaped lights, suspended from the ceiling, create a cool contrast with the 1850s architecture.

Continuing on my tour, I came across a rather rock 'n' roll leather-walled room housing a blue-baize pool table. I am not a big pool man, alas, and was far more interested in some outdoor activity. The 55-acre estate is simply beautiful; I took a six-mile run, cross-country, without coming anywhere close to retracing my steps. The gardens are a superbly cultivated 'wild' expanse, with a lake, and a river flowing under bridges and over a cascade. My next move was towards a massage; Cowley's grounds also contain a no-expense-spared modern spa, all

dark-green slate and glass walls, with wonderful views of the great outdoors, and a range of treatments to rival the best: relaxing, energising, pampering... With its palatial indoor and outdoor pools, this spot was, for me and my girlfriend, the high point of the whole place, and we didn't emerge for some hours.

On a higher plane, post-spa, I was, I must admit, happy to return to the comparative calm of our bedroom; there's only so much cutting-edge design I can take. It was more comfortable than it looked in the brochure and, in true Cowley style, there wasn't an antique in sight: the minimal lines and block colours gave it something of a Swedish feel. The bathroom was the best bit. With its blond woods, limestone double basins and walk-through shower with huge drench head, it was like a mini spa in itself, spacious and luxurious.

Cowley couldn't be more different from my personal vision of comfort and luxury. But it is setting its own agenda, and is very much a place to be discovered. Clearly, the iconoclastic interiors and cocktail-bar atmosphere are aimed at a younger generation raised on a diet of TV design shows; traditionalists may well find themselves slightly bemused by the experience. The staff are unpretentious; the food is good – the chef wisely serves traditional dishes alongside more contemporary cuisine; and the decor has to be seen to be believed. The most enjoyable moment of our stay was the simple pleasure of sitting out on the terrace with a glass of viognier, just taking in our surroundings. Papier-mâché baboons are fun, lime-green armchairs are eye-catching, but I am just as impressed by what a privilege it is to be one of only a handful of people sharing this majestic property in such a beautiful landscape.

Reviewed by Raymond Blanc

Need to know

Rooms 30.

Rates £230–£455, including continental breakfast.

Check-out Midday.

Facilities 55 acres of land, billiards room, spa (the C-Side) with four treatment rooms, indoor and outdoor pools, gym, sauna.

Kids There is a playroom (unsupervised) for kids, and babysitting is available by pre-arrangement. A children's supper is served at 5.30pm (at no extra charge); the hotel asks that the dining room is child-free by 8.30pm.

Also CD and DVD library. Wellington boots are provided.

In the know

Recommended rooms The stable-block rooms, especially the split-level ones. Most Exceptional rooms have own balcony, and the Best room (actual name) has a private terrace, double bath and four-poster bed.

Packing tips Running kit, if you fancy scenic cross-country; swimsuit.

Also Lavender-scented hot-water bottles on request.

Food & drink

In the hotel The grand, oak-panelled dining room is formal but candlelit and welcoming.

Dress code More dressed-down than uptown.

Top table By the window, especially in summer.

Last orders 11pm (10pm during the week).

Room service 24 hours.

Breakfast 8am–11.30am at weekends.

Local restaurants Cheltenham: **Le Champignon Sauvage** (01242 573449) serves English and French cuisine; the **Daffodil** (01242 700055) serves Mod Med, in art deco surrounds.

Local bars **Montpellier Wine Bar** (01242 527774) in regency Cheltenham has a lively atmosphere.

Local pubs The **Hare and Hounds**, Fosse Cross (01285 720288) for delicious gastro food. The **Fossebridge Inn** near Northleach (01285 720721) is ideal for Sunday lunch: book ahead. The 17th-century **Lamb Inn** at Great Rissington (01451 820388) has a great garden.

Worth getting out of bed for

Hot-air ballooning (01242 675003; www.hot-air-ballooning.ltd.uk). Cheltenham races, seven miles away (01242 537642; www.cheltenham.co.uk). Clay-pigeon shooting (01242 870391).

Diary March: Cheltenham Festival starts Britain's horse-racing calendar, and hosts the Gold Cup (01242 537642; www.cheltenham.co.uk). June: The Warwickshire Cup at Cirencester Polo Club (01285 653225). July: Cheltenham's Music and Fringe Festival features music concerts, street entertainment, comedy and fireworks; the Royal International Air Tattoo at RAF Fairford (01285 713300; www.airtattoo.com).

Smith Two complimentary spa products.

Get a room! Check availability and make reservations through www.mrandmrssmith.com.

Cowley Manor Cowley, near Cheltenham, Gloucestershire (01242 870900)
stay@cowleymanor.com; www.cowleymanor.com

past

well

it's

time

bed

your

Didsbury House

S S M T W T F ▪ M T W T F S S M T W T F S S M T W T F S S M T W

Style Manhattan minimalist
Setting Suburban Manchester

it's the characterful
touches that mark the
hotel out as a masterpiece
of modern hospitality

SMTWTFSSMTWTFSSMTWTFSSMTWTFSSMTWTFSSMTW

Didsbury

The more contemporary younger sister of townhouse
hotel Eleven Didsbury Park, Didsbury House is a
£2 million refurbishment of astounding proportions.
It's a grade II-listed Victorian villa and coach-house
knocked into one, featuring twisty-turny staircases, an
imposing stained-glass window over the main stairway,
and unexpected dead ends that give you the feeling
you're having fun in a very grown-up playhouse. It's the
characterful touches that make it so special. Almost
hidden photo albums of holiday snaps of an unknown
family, in-room DVD and CD players, plenty of bathroom
goodies, and tiny jugs of real milk in the fridges mark
Didsbury House out as a masterpiece of modern hospitality.

Because of the house's unconventional layout, each room
has a character of its own; the repeat visitor should aim
at sampling all of them. Room 12 is a split-level condo,
whose Victorian-style overhead shower functions with
Niagara-force vigour. We upgrade to room 52 for our
second night: no contest, it is one of the best rooms we

have ever stayed in, anywhere in the world. Perched in the rafters of the house, it feels more like a New York loft than a hotel room. Here, you can live out any 'millionaire media magnate taking the secretary away for a dirty weekend' fantasies that you might secretly harbour. We can especially recommend having a side-by-side bath in the twin rolltop baths. In the dark. With the in-room CD player on.

The other guests (a designer-clad but unflashy mixture of black-collar creatives and international business types) are happy to share bar chat, but equally willing to leave you locked in a Sunday broadsheet. Staff are equally low-key: friendly without being overbearing, helpful without being servile. And all of them make great late-night bar company. The hotel's zinc-plated elliptical bar, with its stepped drinks display, oozes unforced urban cool. We chose from a decent selection of world-class wines before lunch, picked at a fantastic, fresh

warm-chicken salad at midday, and returned for Courvoisier at 1am. Truthfully, if I'd had my way, we wouldn't have left the bar at all during our two-day stay. The lounge is crowned by a monumental Philippe Starck anglepoise lamp; the whole hotel reminds us of his creative and business muse Ian Schrager's Paramount on New York's West 46th Street. It's a mix of traditional and modern: minimal whites, natural pines, greys and blacks in the hallways and rooms, and deep colours in the lounges and detailing. The lower-ground breakfast room opens out onto a white-walled summer garden.

A stand-out feature of Didsbury House (and extremely rare, in our experience) is its extra-late breakfast service, which runs until the last guest leaves – a true boon to the seasoned hotel whore. Basically, I've never spent a sober night in any hotel anywhere, so the chance to have a good-length lie-in without missing the chance of a freshly cooked Irish

breakfast is almost too good to be true. Black pudding and white, on one plate? Instant hangover cure. And if physical pleasure is your thing, all manner of stimulating face and body treatments are available 30 seconds away from any room in the house, in the subterranean So Spa and gym; plump for a post-breakfast hot-stones treatment (the closest thing you get to an illegal carnal experience in a reputable hotel).

All we knew of Didsbury before this trip is that *Cold Feet* was filmed there, so we were surprised to discover that it's like a cooler, Sloane-free version of London's Holland Park, full of pubs, bars, and impressive restaurants. We tried the Jem & I and the Lime House; both were excellent. The area is packed with good-looking, youngish people out to have a great time, rather than out to impress.

You can see Didsbury House as a genuine break in itself (it's quite tempting not to leave the premises), or as a tranquil base for excursions into Britain's buzzing second city. Either way, two days here feels like a week on holiday. Owners Eamonn and Sally O'Loughlin have created a thoroughly eccentric, decidedly British experience, worthy of an international reputation.

Reviewed by Anthony Noguera

Need to know

Rooms 27, from Classic doubles to Studio Suites.
Rates £135–£300.
Check-out 11am.
Facilities Gym, dry spa with Yon-Ka products, carpark.
Kids Welcome. £25 charge for a child bed.

In the know

Recommended rooms The Studio Suite has twin free-standing baths and a steam room. The Junior Suite has a free-standing bath. Or take one of the split-level rooms (11, 12, 32 and 35).
Packing tips CDs; DVDs for suites.
Also Book spa treatments and Manchester restaurants well in advance.

Food & drink

In the hotel No restaurant. International deli menu in the bar and lounge.
Dress code Laissez-faire.
Top table Both lounges are candlelit at night.
Last orders Service stops when you do.
Room service Deli menu until 10.30pm. There's a night porter later on.
Breakfast From 7am weekdays; 8am weekends, until the last guest has eaten.
Local restaurants **Jem & I** (0161 445 3996) and the **Lime Tree** (0161 445 1217) serve Modern European, and **Casa Tapas** (0161 448 2515) is close to the hotel. In Manchester, the **Restaurant Bar and Grill** (0161 839 1999) and **Le Mont** (0161 605 8282).
Local bars The hotel can arrange guestlist for VIP rooms at **Tiger Tiger** (0161 385 8080) and the **Living Room** (0161 832 0083). The **Circle Club** in Manchester (0161 288 8118).
Local pubs The **Metropolitan** (0161 374 9559) has a great restaurant and a huge garden.

Worth getting out of bed for

Old Trafford is a 15-minute drive away. The Peak District, for a fix of country air. The hotel can organise tickets for the Opera House and the Palace Theatre (www.manchestertheatres.co.uk). Lyme Park is a stunning National Trust stately home, with mountain biking and pony trekking. Greyhound racing (www.bellevuestadium.co.uk). Classical music at Bridgewater Hall (www.bridgewater-hall.co.uk). Shopping includes Harvey Nichols, Selfridges, DKNY, Joseph and Armani.
Diary August: Mardi Gras (www.manchestermardigras.com). October: Manchester Food & Drink Festival (www.foodanddrinkfestival.com).

 Smith A free glass of champagne with breakfast.

Get a room! Check availability and make reservations through www.mrandmrssmith.com.

Didsbury House Didsbury Park, Didsbury Village, Manchester (0161 448 2200)
enquiries@didsburyhouse.co.uk; www.didsburyhouse.co.uk

Driftwood

Style New England yacht club
Setting Bracing Cornish clifftop

Rosevine

WTFSSMTWTFSSMTWTFSSMTWTFSSMTWTFSSMTWTFS

both accessible and remote

Driftwood has been open for just long enough to be used to stressed-out urban types like us pouring out of our cars demanding gin. When we arrived, owners Paul and Fiona Robinson were there to welcome us. Both of them serene and efficient, they immediately began the challenging process of getting us relaxed.

Striking the perfect balance between accessible and remote, the main house has an incredible setting, high on a cliff with spectacular views over the bay and Driftwood's own private beach. From the outside it doesn't look out of the ordinary, but the interior has been given a great deal of thought: the furnishings have a comfortable, homely feel, in blues and creams and natural woods – all very, very tasteful. With only a few rooms to choose from, we were extremely lucky to have booked the prize one: the Cabin, a proper little Tom Sawyer house a short stagger from the main property. Perched halfway down the cliffs, it's nicely secluded, with its own cosy sitting room, and steamer chairs out front. There are two bedrooms – a double and a twin – so you can bring the kids if you have them or, as we did, just spread out.

There are few hotel philosophies more appealing than 'nothing is too much trouble', and this place goes by exactly that. Whether you would like a massage booked or a picnic packed for you, Paul and Fiona will see to it; Driftwood offers a very personal service that is always unobtrusive. They even let us borrow their dog Buffy for a little stick-throwing on the fantastic private beach (they got the dog back, but we never saw the stick again).

As you might expect with such a glorious bay visible just beyond the window of the restaurant, Driftwood's speciality is seafood. The menu is all fantastic; people travel miles to sample fresh fish, locally reared meat and predominantly organic creations. The Robinsons are perfectly understanding of those after a romantic escape; they organise an early supper sitting for kids and, with the children's games room away from the main house, there is always a calm, relaxed atmosphere. There's also a sitting room to kick back in, with a wide hearth for the cooler months and a bar area next to the dining room. Diners make a bit of an effort with their dress; it's a Ralph Lauren country-casual feel (this didn't stop Mrs Smith wearing her heels).

Having fallen asleep to the soporific sound of waves crashing onto the beach, we slept soundly and late. When I eventually flung open the cabin door I was greeted by a playful-looking Buffy. Making the mistake of inviting her into the cabin, I watched helplessly as she sidled up to the side of the bed, seized a pair of Agent Provocateur's finest and departed. 'Fetch!' I was instructed by Mrs Smith, and I sallied forth, discovering along the way that whatever breed Buffy is, it isn't of the slow and stupid variety. A merry dance ensued resulting in me poorer to the tune of one pair of knickers.

A 20-minute amble along the coastal path brought us to the nearby fishing village of Portscatho for a pint and a pasty in the Plume of Feathers, a great local boozer. Down the road we stumbled across the Gallery Portscatho, an artists' collective that is well worth a visit, run by the friendly Chris Insoll. He was more than happy to show us round, and we were able to pick up some bargains from the upstairs studio before they were shipped off for sale in London.

Paul had very wisely booked us a table at the Green Lantern for more fine seafood. Later on, we tarried a little in the Driftwood bar and took a bottle of pinot noir back to our candlelit porch. Naturally, we woke craving tasty food. And we weren't disappointed. After wolfing down scrambled eggs and smoked salmon, fruit salad and freshly baked bread with home-made marmalade, we retreated to the cabin with the papers until check-out time. Since there was no one booked in after us, we were allowed to stay in our little hideaway until early afternoon – Fiona even made us an afternoon tea to take away with us. The fruitcake alone ensured our Driftwood experience kept us satisfied until we reached home.

Reviewed by Mr & Mrs Smith

Need to know

Rooms 14 rooms, and a private cabin overlooking the beach.
Rates £160–£200, including breakfast, morning paper and, in low season, dinner.
Check-out 11am.
Facilities Private beach, seven acres of heritage coastline.
Kids Warmly welcomed. There is a £10 charge for under-12s sharing parents' room and a £15 charge for over-12s; this includes breakfast. The games room includes a PlayStation.
Also No smoking throughout.

In the know

Recommended rooms The Cabin has two bedrooms and offers perfect seclusion. Room 10 is the largest room, with a fantastic view of Gerrans Bay.
Packing tips Frisbee, kite, binoculars.
Also The kitchen will provide a picnic hamper on request.

Food & drink

In the hotel Fresh, local and organic ingredients; wonderful fish and seafood.
Dress code Chino chic and deck shoes.
Top table A conservatory table, overlooking the sea.
Last orders Food: 9.30pm.
Room service Staff will accommodate special requests.
Breakfast 8am–10.30am; until 10am on Sundays.
Local restaurants The **Lugger** in Portloe (01872 501322; see page 122) does excellent seafood. The **Hotel Tresanton** in St Mawes (01326 270055; see page 196) has superb organic food.
Local pubs The **Roseland Inn** in Philleigh (01872 580254) does fantastic Sunday lunches, worth booking ahead for. The **Plume of Feathers** in Portscatho (01872 580321) for lunch and a pint.

Worth getting out of bed for

A stomp along the cliff paths for a pint in Portscatho. A trip to the National Maritime Museum in Falmouth (01326 313388; www.nmmc.co.uk); the foot ferry leaves St Mawes Harbour every 20 minutes. Tate St Ives (01736 796226; www.tate.org.uk/stives). The Eden Project (01726 811911; www.edenproject.com). The Extreme Academy, Newquay (01637 860840; www.watergatebay.co.uk) has the UK's only ski resort on a beach and also organises waterskiing, windsurfing and more. The Gallery Portscatho (01872 580719).
Diary July/August Newquay Surf Festival (www.britsurf.co.uk). August: Falmouth Classics Regatta Week. October: Falmouth Oyster Festival for oyster tasting, washed down with champagne and Guinness.

Smith A free bottle of house wine with your evening meal.

Get a room! Check availability and make reservations through www.mrandmrssmith.com.

Driftwood Rosevine, near Portscatho, Cornwall (01872 580644)
info@driftwoodhotel.co.uk; www.driftwoodhotel.co.uk

it only takes a brisk ten-minute walk along the shores of windermere before
we find ourselves drawn back towards the homely confines of the duck

The Drunken Duck Inn

M T W T F S S M T W T ⬭ M T W T F S S M T W T F S S M T W T F S S M T W T F

Style Top-notch traditional pub

Setting Stunning Cumbrian hills

Barngates

MTWTFSSMTWTFSSMTWTFSSMTW

'nothing's this far off
the beaten track, darling'

If Jemima Puddleduck had ever gone on a romantic weekend, this is what the Beatrix Potter illustration would have looked like: a cream 19th-century inn, tucked away in idyllic countryside. When we finally find the Drunken Duck ('Nothing's this far off the beaten track, darling' – a few interrogated ramblers and a handful of 'I told you so's later, we discover it is) we are transformed from marriage-guidance candidates into characters from a Doris Day movie. 'Honey, it's perfect,' I exclaim.

The manager shows us to our room in the hotel wing behind the pub, through a sunny hall packed with boardgames and books. The rooms, each of which has its own distinct personality, are contemporary in decor, with antiques here and there. What takes our breath away is the view of rolling countryside, punctuated only by flowering hedgerows and a small tarn; if only John Constable were still around to paint it. Personal touches in our room include a shelf full of books, a few of which are definitely on my should-read list. Then we remember that our intentions at the Duck involved fresh air and the great outdoors. Well, maybe after a swift half.

The Drunken Duck has its own brewery, Barngate, where you can sample a Cat Nap bitter or a Chesters Strong and Ugly ale, either inside the cosy pub or at a table outside. Over our first pint, having discovered that all the brews are named after pets from days gone by, we enquire as to how the pub got its name. 'It dates back to Victorian times,' the barman tells us. 'The landlady found her ducks sprawled outside on the road so, assuming they were dead, she chucked a pan of orange sauce on the hob and got on with plucking the poor souls. A few ruffled feathers later, she discovered they weren't dead at all, but half-cut – a beer barrel had leaked its contents into their watering hole.'

The temptation is to spend all day in the snug catching up on local lore, but with everyone around us wearing hiking boots, we are inspired to work up an appetite for dinner. A brisk walk along Windermere does the trick; ten minutes later we find ourselves drawn back towards the homely confines of the Duck. Too early to pitch up for dinner, we decide to take a quick boat trip around Lake Windermere. The tours here come in all shapes and sizes throughout the day; we find an hour-long cruise that suits us fine, allowing us to get back to the inn for afternoon tea in the resident's garden.

The pub is very small and wonderfully traditional, with a stuffed fox mounted on the wall and beamed ceilings decorated with dried hops. Our fellow drinkers are a mixture of hotel guests up for the weekend and locals enjoying a tipple before being seated in the restaurant. Because the Duck is so popular for dinner, when you book a room the management, quite rightly, reserve you a table automatically.

The food cannot be faulted, and the fabulous wine list has delightfully wordy descriptions to help you pick just the right one. The menu is an adventurous take on traditional favourites, with an emphasis on quality rather than quantity. There's a decent selection for every course, though the sea-bass and local lamb are particularly good; just don't think about the little woolly fellows grazing outside your window. When bedtime comes we certainly aren't counting sheep: our bed is up there with the world's most comfortable. On waking, we snuggle into the duvet and plump pillows, dreaming of being able to stay a few days longer. As the fresh breeze blows in from the open patio door, we're soon calculating how long work can do without us. Then we remember breakfast. Never has there been a better reason to get out of bed. Freshly squeezed orange and raspberry juice, a range of hearty options from pancakes to full English – even the marmalade is incredible. It turns out to be harder to leave the Drunken Duck than it was to find it.

Reviewed by Mr & Mrs Smith

Need to know

Rooms 16.
Rates £95–£210, including breakfast.
Check-out 11am.
Facilities There is a small fishing tarn, with trout and fly-fishing rights between March and September, and a private garden for residents.
Also No smoking in the restaurant, but it is permitted in the bar.
Kids There are no family rooms, but the restaurant will provide children's portions.

In the know

Recommended rooms Room 17 (the Garden Room) and Room 11 for the view.
Rooms 1, 12, 15 and 16 have their own patios.
Packing tips Walking shoes, Ordnance Survey map, fishing rod. Bring your own VHS videos.
Also Umbrellas provided.

Food & drink

In the hotel The restaurant attracts visitors from miles around for its legendary pub lunches and Modern English menu, which features local produce wherever possible.
Dress code Think wild and windy; smarter for dinner.
Top table Any window table.
Last orders Food: 9.15pm (pre-arrange for any later). Pub licensing laws apply for drinking; a night porter will cater for residents after 11pm.
Room service Only for breakfast in bed.
Breakfast 8.30am–10am.
Local restaurants The highly acclaimed family-run **Jericho's** in Windermere (01539 442522). The **Glasshouse** for Modern British food in Ambleside (01539 432137). **L'Enclume** (01539 536362; see page 102) is a 45-minute drive away, but well worth the journey for lunch.
Local pubs The **Queen's Head** at Troutbeck (01539 432174) for trad pub grub and great views.

Worth getting out of bed for

If the views don't get you out of bed, nothing will; a drive across the Hardnott Pass is a must for the hairy corners and fantastic panoramas. Get touristy at the Steamboat Museum (01539 445565), which organises daily outings on Lake Windermere. For water sports on Lake Windermere, such as sailing, canoeing, kayaking and boat hire, go to www.lakedistrictletsgo.co.uk/watersports.
Diary August: Grasmere Sports, including wrestling, terrier racing and tug of war (01539 432127; www.grasmeresports.co.uk) October: Vale of Rydal Sheepdog Trials, with show-jumping for Jack Russells (01539 432321; www.heartofthelakes.co.uk).

Smith Afternoon tea and cakes for two in Chester's Coffee Shop at Touchstone Interiors.

Get a room! Check availability and make reservations through www.mrandmrssmith.com.

The Drunken Duck Inn Barngates, Ambleside, Cumbria (01539 436347)
info@drunkenduckinn.co.uk; www.drunkenduckinn.co.uk

L'Enclume

M T W T F ■ M T W T F S S M T W T F S S M T W T F S S

Style Temple to haute cuisine
Setting Hidden village in the Lakes

Cartmel

WTFSSMTWTFSSMTWTFSSMTWTFSSMTWTFSSMTWTFS

one of the finest restaurants in the country, and if you're smart you book one of their fantastic rooms to roll into after dinner

Our afternoon jaunt up to Cartmel didn't run as smoothly as we'd hoped. Owing to an ill-starred encounter between Mrs Smith and a savage bee, a brief diversion to Kendal General Hospital was needed. While the helpful folk in the A&E department were super-efficient (were we reviewing for *Dr & Nurse Smith*, we'd thoroughly recommend it), the true healer was the prospect of a night at L'Enclume.

Hidden at the heart of a village in the Lake District, it took some magnified map reading to find. Diametrically opposed to a motorway Travelodge in the easy-to-find stakes, it is also joyfully far removed from such establishments in the food department. L'Enclume is one of the finest restaurants in the country, and if you're smart you book one of their fantastic rooms to roll into after dinner.

It's appropriate that the restaurant front-of-house doubles as the hotel reception, since this place is all about the comestibles. Here we were met by Stephen, the master sommelier, who greeted us by name and, taking our car keys in case the owner of the gleaming Maserati we had blocked in needed to get out, showed us to our bedroom. Spacious and comfortable, it was stylishly decorated with toile de Jouy wallpaper, with matching curtains and a compact but fully equipped ensuite bathroom.

Since we'd been advised that it's best to arrive by 7pm for the nine-course menu gourmand, we went down for an early aperitif in the garden. A few amuse-bouches were enough to get us salivating, and we braced ourselves for a two-and-a-half-hour journey of the tastebuds. I even persuaded a slightly reluctant Stephen (concerned for our budget) to recommend wines that would complement our food and he chose perfectly, while also demonstrating great diplomacy.

L'Enclume's reputation for fine dining is anything but pie in the sky. When the food arrived, artistically presented in an array of glass vessels, we realised we were about to consume the work of a genius. Such is chef and owner Simon Rogan's passion for cooking that his only two days off in the previous 12 months had been to visit his culinary hero's

restaurants in France: Marc Veyrat's L'Auberge de l'Eridane in Annecy, and La Ferme de Mon Père in Megève. Simon certainly deserves to match Veyrat's Michelin-star status, and his ultimate aim is to offer the full dining experience as he sees it: a 16-course menu. He champions organic produce, and works with local producers to bring the highest-quality ingredients to the table. The foodstuffs are, indeed, the finest imaginable, the combinations unconventional, and the results unforgettable. The staff are efficient, charming and polite – especially admirable in such a temple to haute cuisine, which could otherwise feel a little intimidating. The light, airy and contemporary surroundings were the perfect environment for such a gastronomic extravaganza: the centrepiece was an old blacksmith's anvil – the *enclume* that this lovely place is named after.

I felt a little underdressed at dinner in a sweater and slacks, but in the morning I was assured I hadn't broken any house rules. Seated at a table in the conservatory, we enjoyed a leisurely breakfast of porridge with home-made syrup before taking a tour of our locale. The first thing to catch our eye was an exquisite sofa in the window of Anthemian Antiques, the shop responsible for the interior of L'Enclume. Cartmel may seem an unlikely place to find a £12,000 sofa, but then you wouldn't necessarily expect to stumble on a world-class restaurant there, either. Tempted as I was by the Louis XV couch, sanity prevailed. Wallets intact, we took a look around the 12th-century Cartmel Priory and ended up at the village shop for elevenses. It's a tourist attraction in its own right, so the Johns family told us, for its sticky toffee pudding. As we tucked into a serving, one of the clan (after informing us that Madonna is also a big fan) observed that it was our first visit. 'Ah, you'll be back for more. They always are...' He smiled knowingly, making it sound a little as though we'd joined a cult. And maybe we had. Even with the Cartmel Village Shop Original Sticky Toffee Pudding stocked in Fortnum & Mason, it's hard to imagine we won't be. There aren't many villages that leave quite such a good taste in your mouth.

Reviewed by Oliver Tress

Need to know

Rooms Four traditional rooms, one suite, two contemporary garden rooms (interconnecting).

Rates £125–£200, including breakfast.

Check-out 11am, but flexible.

Kids No under-10s in the dining room at night.

Also No smoking.

In the know

Recommended rooms Trouvé, the biggest room. Beaumont Suite and Fletcher Suite each have separate seating areas. Priory View Room.

Packing tips Anything with an elasticated waistband.

Food & drink

In the hotel Spectacular modern French food, using local and sometimes wild ingredients.

Dress code Understated smart.

Top table Alfresco, or with view over garden and priory.

Last orders Lunch: 1.30pm. Dinner: 9.15pm. No bar.

Room service At management's discretion.

Breakfast 9am–10am.

Local restaurants The **Drunken Duck** in Barngate (01539 436347; see page 96) is a great traditional inn. The **Glasshouse** for Modern British food in Ambleside (01539 432137).

Local pubs The **Masons Arms** at Cartmel Fell (01539 568486) and the **Queen's Head** at Troutbeck (01539 432174) both serve good food.

Also The **Cartmel Village Shop** (01539 536201; www.sticky-toffee-pudding.co.uk) is a well-stocked delicatessen that is legendary for its sticky toffee pudding.

Worth getting out of bed for

Parachuting at North West Parachute Centre (01539 558672; www.skydive23.freeserve.co.uk). Fishing at Bigland Waters (01539 531728; www.where-to-fish.com). Water sports on Lake Windermere (www.lakedistrictletsgo.co.uk/watersports). Hot-air-balloon rides over the lakes (www.high-adventure.co.uk). Walking the Cumbrian coastal way.

Diary May and August bank holidays: steeplechase races (01539 586340) at Cartmel, the smallest and most scenic of the north-west racetracks. August: Grasmere Sports, including wrestling, terrier racing and tug of war (01539 432127; www.grasmeresports.co.uk). October: Windermere Powerboat Records (01539 443284; www.rya.org.uk/powerboating).

Get a room! Check availability and make reservations through www.mrandmrssmith.com.

Cavendish Street, Cartmel, Cumbria (01539 536362)
enquiries@lenclume.co.uk; www.lenclume.co.uk

Hotel du Vin

Style **Wine-lovers' world of their own**

Setting **Yards from Brighton's seafront**

a bubble of comfort you can lose yourself in, rain or shine

Brighton

SSMTWTFSSMTWTFSSMTWTFSSMTWTFSSMTWTFS

Ah, Brighton on a summer's day. We're thinking salty air, giggles on the pier, a stroll on the beach hand in hand… but it's lashing it down and the umbrella's inside out before we've decided whether to make a dash for the pub or the shops. Happily, the heart of this seaside town is so walkable that we haven't managed to wander far from base. The Hotel du Vin is rather less English and definitely less predictable than the weather. A gothicky, Thirties-built château, yards from the seafront, it has a sea-green exterior, just the colour of the Channel (visible at the end of the street). It's a bubble of comfort that you can lose yourself in, rain or shine. And, although it's heaven for wine-lovers, you don't have to know your chardonnay from your Châteauneuf-du-Pape to feel at home.

We took one of the smaller rooms, Gracia de Chile (each room is named after a different wine house). It was modern and comfortable, with fresh Egyptian-cotton bedlinen; the free-standing bath and enormous shower were particularly fun-inspiring. Had we wanted to spend more time getting to know one another, however, we would have chosen either Gosset or Cristal, where twin baths, gorgeous sea views and salubrious amounts of space are more seductive than a magnum of either of the above.

The decking area outside our room looked inviting enough, even in the drizzle – just right for a spot of casual minibar abuse in the evening sun.

The bar, on the ground floor of the hotel, is an airy double-height space decorated in chocolate browns, with a buzzy but laid-back vibe. Happily sunk into one of the sofas, we could have watched the world go by all night: one side is all shelves, filled with wine books; high on the opposite wall, a louche mural tells a tale or two. After pouncing on bowls of olives and nuts, we chose our first bottle from the 600-bin wine list, and took our table in the Bistro. The restaurant has decidedly French leanings, with banquettes and bronzes, and wine-related prints, photographs and maps covering the walls. Among ex-ravers, arty locals and happy tourists, we were fed handsomely; I was most impressed with the sommelier, especially when he recommended the cheaper one of two reds we were dithering between, saying it had 'more personality'. There is a private dining room in the cellar – perhaps a mite claustrophobic for some, but after a few bottles of Vacqueyras, you'd get over it. If you feel like staying up all night, Brighton's no slouch; we considered a drink at pre-club cocktail haunt Koba (beware – with just a discreet plaque to announce itself, it's hard to find) but decided, as most guests do, that we couldn't bring ourselves to stray seriously from our new home away from home.

Breakfast was wonderful – so hearty we could have
done with a lie-down afterwards. (Be warned: it is not
included in the price of the room, but it is worth
the splurge.) The sun was shining though, so we hit the
Lanes. We were both familiar with Brighton's holistic
hippie vibe (you still get the odd whiff of patchouli
wafting out of doorways), but found plenty to tempt
our less tie-dye tastes: round the corner from the hotel
we found the most fantastic toyshop we've ever seen, a
whole row of little silversmiths, and countless funky
boutiques, as well as all the usual names. The staff at
the hotel had recommended La Fourchette in
Montpellier for lunch, but we were still doing quite well
on Galway bacon and black pudding, so a pint seemed
the natural way to take a break from our wanderings.
The Regency Tavern on Russell Square is the sort of
pub everyone should have as their local. It's full of every
kind of people – gay, straight, young, old – and has a
theatrical art deco elegance. After that longed-for walk
along the beach we were happy to head back to the
haven of the Hotel du Vin. It's a definite contrast to
Brighton's anarchic personality, a world away from
kitsch and kiss-me-quick. The wine list was calling, the
charming waiters were waiting. One word of advice: don't
check in at the Hotel du Vin if you've got a hangover –
come here to get one.

Reviewed by Mr & Mrs Smith

Need to know

Rooms 37 rooms, including two junior suites, one loft suite.
Rates From £115; junior suites, from £185. The loft suite costs
£250 on weekdays, £350 at weekends.
Check-out 11am weekdays; 11.30am weekends (extended on request).
Kids Baby-listening, babysitting and nannies need to be booked in advance.
Also Smoking allowed in restaurant; pipes and cigars in bar only.

In the know

Recommended rooms The Gosset and Louis Roederer suites in particular, but all suites
have a sea view, telescope and side-by-side baths. Cristal has an eight-foot-square bed.
Packing tips Beach hat, Alka Seltzer and rubber duck.
Also Ring ahead to book for connoisseur wine evenings at the hotel.

Food & drink

In the hotel Eclectic Modern European food: wine-lovers very well catered for.
Dress code Low-key dressy.
Top table A window seat.
Last orders Kitchen closes at 9.45pm; bar open all night for guests.
Room service Continental breakfast in bed. Drinks available all night.
Breakfast 7am–10am weekdays, 8am–11am weekends.
Local restaurants **7 Dials** for Modern British (01273 885555). French cuisine at
La Fourchette (01273 722556). The **Gingerman** (01273 326688) for Euro gastro.
Joogleberry Playhouse (01273 687171) serves the most mouth-watering tapas at
affordable prices, while downstairs they have a cabaret bar which offers live entertainment
nightly, in a smoky jazz club environment. For more information, go to www.joogleberry.com
Local bars **Koba** (01273 720059) for cocktails, or better still, **Heist** on West Street (01273
822555). Dress up for the **Ebony Room** (01273 675007) on the Marina. The **Funky
Buddha Lounge** (01273 725541) shuts at 3am.
Local pubs The **Hop Poles** (01273 710444) and the **Eagle Bar & Bakery** (01273 710444)
both have great food. The **Regency Tavern** (01273 325652) for a pint in art deco surrounds.

Worth getting out of bed for

Get strapped to an instructor at the Paragliding and Hang-gliding Club in Glynde (01273
858108). Hove Lagoon Watersports for all water activities, including kite-surfing (01273
424842). On a rainy day, get into Sixties mod culture at the Brighton Museum & Art Gallery.
Diary May to August: Glyndebourne Opera, a ten-minute drive away near Lewes (01273
813813; www.glyndebourne.com). First week November: London to Brighton Veteran Car
Run (01753 681736; www.msauk.org).

Smith A complimentary bottle of house champagne.

Get a room! Check availability and make reservations through www.mrandmrssmith.com.

Hotel du Vin Ship Street, Brighton (01273 718588)
info@brightonhotelduvin.com; www.hotelduvin.com

throw a frisbee...

throw a frisbee...

How to...

The throw explained below is known as the CLASSIC. This is the easiest throw to master and is the Frisbee equivalent of the tennis backhand.

STEP 1: THE HOLD Loosely grip the Frisbee with your thumb on the top and your four fingers in the rim underneath.

STEP 2: THE STANCE If you're right-handed, stand at an angle to the receiver, with your right foot and right shoulder towards them. (If you're left-handed... well, figure it out.)

STEP 3: THE WIND-UP Wind your throwing arm in towards your body at chest height, curling your wrist in slightly. Keep your feet rooted and pivot your body at the hips, turning your front shoulder away from the receiver. Like a coiled spring, you're now ready to throw...

STEP 4: THE THROW As with most 'throwing sports', aim is always more accurate if one keeps an eye on where one wants to throw. Keeping the Frisbee horizontal, whip your throwing arm out towards the receiver. At the last point of the throw, uncurl your wrist. This gives the Frisbee the flick it needs to keep it spinning.

You'll get better accuracy and distance if you keep STEP 3 and STEP 4 as a fluid motion. As always, practice makes perfect.

...throw a frisbee...
...throw a frisbee...

The Ickworth Hotel

when the tourists make their way
home, you can't help but feel a
little smug when you stay behind
to wine, dine and sleep over

S S M T W T F ▢ M T W T F S S M T W T F S S M T W

Style Georgian stately home from home
Setting National Trust parkland

Bury St Edmunds

SSMTWTFSSMTWTFSSMTWTFSSMTWTFSSMTWTFSSMT

Whoever sent a Hong Kong-born Chinaman, who owns a number of bars and nightclubs in London, to review a grand country-house hotel in the heart of Suffolk, did so with a smile on their face. The Chinese are not renowned for their Range Rovers, Barbour jackets or green wellies. And to make matters worse, the nearest casino was 40 miles away. Clearly, there were plans for me to be the joker in the pack.

With impressive gates and a quarter-mile drive up to the hotel, few entrances can be grander than the one to Ickworth House. The hotel is located in the east wing of a National Trust property open to the public, and the gardens attract a steady stream of visitors from every generation. When the tourists make their way home at the end of the day, you can't help but feel a little smug. As a guest, you get to stay behind to wine, dine and sleep over.

To a lord or a duke, this place might seem like a home from home: quaint, charming, friendly and efficient. It also has enough of a contemporary twist to keep the *Wallpaper** crowd happy. Judging by the guestbook, the vast majority of those who come to stay are mainly, like us, young families from London. The room names hark back to the history of the building (Lady Elizabeth, Lord Augustine). We were allocated the Nursery – appropriate, since our companions for the weekend included our daughters, Olivia, 12, and Tamara, ten. It was a good size, with double bed, sofabed and smart TVs with built-in DVD/CD player.

With such a magnificent property at our disposal, we prayed the rain would stay away. The bicycles provided allowed us to explore and admire Ickworth's 1,800-acre grounds. But the girls' favourite part of the weekend was having a splash in the swimming pool. Though it's charming that the rest of the hotel is steeped in history, that's hardly what you want in this department; located in a modern annexe off the hotel, the pool is terrifically clean, with two glass walls allowing the sunshine to penetrate.

When we booked for dinner, the receptionist came back with a table-for-two reservation in Frederick's, suggesting the children would prefer the other eatery. It's great having time away as a family, but also wonderful to enjoy parts of it as a couple. Café Inferno is about what children like, rather than aesthetics. Located in the basement, it has a cafeteria feel; it's likely to be where the nanny and the kids tuck into

their burger and chips while the parents indulge themselves in the two wood-panelled rooms that form Frederick's upstairs. (The hotel offers a baby-listening service for couples who brought the kids but still want a romantic experience). Here, the gentlemen's-club atmosphere – lots of cutlery and big glasses and well-turned-out staff – make it feel like a grand occasion: fine dining, Modern European-style, and an excellent wine list that made a 1995 Château Musar irresistible.

Though there is no bar as such – nowhere you can lean against and impress the barman with your knowledge of Scottish malts – there are two beautiful lounges decorated with an incredible array of art deco furniture where waitresses come and take your drinks orders. I got the distinct impression that no one chooses Ickworth for a wild weekend, so don't bother packing your Dolce & Gabbana. This is a place for families and happily attached couples wanting somewhere to hide and relax. And how...

Tennis courts and stables were among the possibilities the following morning, but it was the spa that won the toss. It isn't huge, but I enjoyed one of the best massages ever (ask for the Italian lady). It was the icing on the cake for the Chinaman who just wanted to see how it felt to be lord of the manor for the weekend. All that was lacking was the ability to end my visit with the words 'Bring the Bentley round will you, James?'. Maybe next time.

Reviewed by Eric Yu

Need to know

Rooms 27 rooms and 11 apartments.
Rates £175–£535, including breakfast.
Check-out 11am.
Facilities 1,800 acres of parkland, with woods and lakes (quad-bike tours and horse-riding can be arranged), tennis courts, indoor pool and spa and three treatment rooms.
Kids Playroom, creche, adventure playgrounds, bikes and nature trails. Many rooms are interconnecting or have special child-friendly features; this is *the* hotel to take your children to.
Also No smoking throughout, apart from in one lounge room. Wellies provided. Guests receive free tickets to the National Trust part of the house.

In the know

Recommended rooms Ask for a view over the grounds, and specify if you would prefer a traditional or contemporary feel. Both are lovely.
Packing tips Swimming costumes, outdoor-activity gear.
Also Book a babysitter or nanny in advance if you want to leave the grounds without your offspring.

Food & drink

In the hotel Frederick's is the fine-dining restaurant, where children are only allowed for Sunday lunch. The Conservatory is great for lunch or tea. Café Inferno has a special kids' menu.
Dress code Dress up for dinner at Frederick's; otherwise, casual is fine.
Top table A window seat overlooking the Italian garden.
Last orders Frederick's: 9.30pm. Café Inferno: 9pm. Bar open all night.
Room service Full menu during kitchen hours, cold snacks all night.
Breakfast 7.30am–10am.
Local restaurants The **Great House** at Lavenham (01787 247431) serves French food.
Local pubs The **Beehive** at Horringer (01284 735260) is just at the end of the hotel drive, has a garden, and does great pub food.

Worth getting out of bed for

Newmarket racecourse (www.newmarketracecourses.co.uk). Ring 01638 667200 (www.newmarketexperience.co.uk) for a fully organised race day, or guided tour of a training yard.
Diary July: Newmarket Nights consists of evening races on Fridays, followed by live music (www.newmarketnights.co.uk). October: Champion's Day at Newmarket (01638 663482; www.newmarketracecourses.co.uk). November: Open Pit Lane at Snetterton Race Circuit (01953 887303; www.brandshatchcircuits.co.uk).

 A free bottle of house champagne and a private viewing of the Italian gardens.

Get a room! Check availability and make reservations through www.mrandmrssmith.com.

The Ickworth Hotel Horringer, Bury St Edmunds, Suffolk (01284 735350)
info@ickworthhotel.com; www.luxuryfamilyhotels.com

The Lugger Hotel

S S M T W T F S S M T W T F ▪ M T W T F S S M T W T F S S M T

Style Smuggler's inn turned boutique hideaway
Setting Cornwall's mystical coast

the rooms are lovely, simple and elegant: armani by the sea

Portloe

FSSMTWTFSSMTWTF**SS**MTWTFSSMTWTFSSMTWTFSS

The maidens (my wife and an equally beautiful friend of ours) and I left town at half three on a Friday afternoon and headed towards the sunset and the south-west. We did get lost once, not having a map, a sense of direction or a sane person in the car. For clarity's sake, stay on the road that claims to be the M5 all the way to the A390, and then turn off towards St Austell; do not be distracted by A30s or A38s – they are false gods.

As always, we were late for dinner. The chef at the Lugger Hotel hangs up his hat at a fashionably early 9pm, but he knew we were coming, and had agreed to hold on. The three of us were gently ushered to a corner table overlooking the tiny harbour, and given menus and suggestions. The restaurant is all cool whites and creams, dark-oak beams, honey-hued wooden floors, terracotta tiles and elegant rattan chairs. It made quite a backdrop for the girls. The same minimalist elements have been used throughout the hotel, mixed with a more relaxed, traditional country feel; in a lovely warm library next to the restaurant, books and videos can be browsed by the fireside, over a decent Bloody Mary.

The bar is really part of the restaurant and, therefore, not somewhere to hang out. The restaurant itself would be equally at home in Sydney or Long Island. The food is more than good, the fish spectacular, and the helpful staff a mix of city chic and French au pair. My only complaint would be that the maidens were not on a diet, so when they'd eaten their dinners, they then ate mine, ordered another main course, ate that, and still looked at me expectantly.

Our rooms were in a separate building just behind the hotel, overlooking the village and the sea. (Guests in the main building have harbour and sea views, too.) We took adjacent Deluxe and Classic rooms, sampling the top and bottom end of the scale. They were both lovely, simple and elegant: Armani by the sea. The beds are, if anything, oversized for the rooms, giving a lovely cosy feeling. The Italian cotton sheets and voluptuous pillows get nine out of ten; I would gladly have spent the whole weekend in bed, if I had been allowed to. Being rather dissolute, we missed the 10am deadline for the Full Monty in bed, but hotel rules were bent once again, and we were delivered a wonderful compromise that qualified as an early lunch. Guilt finally set in when I realised that the chambermaids had patiently waited outside for hours, without a word.

Portloe is a working fishing village, replete with lobster pots and nets drying in the wind. It seems to have forced its way into a crack in the coastline, and clings to the rocks like a limpet. It is truly tiny, the hotel sharing the beach with four or five fishing boats and their boatyard. Whitewashed slate-roofed cottages nestle into the hillsides behind the harbour, sheltering from the Atlantic breeze and crashing waves. It is very pretty, very Cornish. The only pub, the Ship Inn is cosy and fun, and its kitchen serves great pub food. The natives seemed friendly: a mixture of villagers and walkers down from the wilds above. The clifftops offer lovely walks and drama-filled views over the ocean, and the countryside approaching the coast is sublime, with the village of Veryan, a few miles away, a dead ringer for Rivendell. We were particularly taken by a building that looked so like a witch's house, with bulbous walls and a fat, squashy look, that we couldn't help chuckling when we saw it.

The Lugger is perfect for brand-new affairs, getting away from the children, and breaking up. You won't want to do much except soak up the atmosphere. This is a place where you can contemplate the past and the future undisturbed, not just because you'll find your mobile won't work, but also because the Lugger does what it does so damn so well.

Reviewed by Rory Keegan

Need to know

Rooms 21, all ensuite.
Rates £200–£240, including breakfast.
Check-out 11am.
Facilities Massage and therapy room, offering reiki, reflexology, Indian head massage and facials.
Kids No children under 12.

In the know

Recommended rooms Rooms 301, 302 and 303 have terraces and the best sea views.
Packing tips Fishing nets, walking boots, Ordnance Survey map.
Also Bring wet-weather gear; when the weather closes in, it really closes in.

Food & drink

In the hotel Restaurant specialising in seafood.
Dress code More dash than flash.
Top table At lunchtime, on the terrace; in the evening, one by the window.
Last orders 9pm (later by pre-arrangement). Bar opening hours are flexible.
Room service Breakfast and drinks only.
Breakfast 8am–10am.
Local restaurants Rick Stein's foodie empire is an hour's drive away in Padstow, but worth the trip (01841 532700; www.rickstein.com). A few miles along the coast in St Mawes is the **Hotel Tresanton** (01326 270055; see page 196) for superb local and organic food. The **Driftwood** (01872 580644; see page 88) for wonderful fish and seafood.
Local pubs In Portloe itself, opposite the hotel, is the **Ship Inn**, which serves good pub food (01872 501356). The **New Inn** in Veryan has a slightly less traditional menu (01872 501362).

Worth getting out of bed for

The bay is great for a refreshing dip (watch out for the lobster pots) or a bracing coastal walk. Tate St Ives (01736 796226; www.tate.org.uk/stives) is a gallery worth visiting. The Eden Project (01726 811911; www.edenproject.com) is an experimental biosphere with the largest conservatories in the world. In high season, get tickets through the hotel to avoid queuing. A trip to the National Maritime Museum in Falmouth (01326 313388; www.nmmc.co.uk); the foot ferry leaves St Mawes Harbour every 20 minutes.
Diary May: there are May Day celebrations in St Ives, Padstow and throughout Cornwall (www.cornishlight.co.uk/cornish-customs.htm). July: Rip Curl Newquay Boardmasters is the UK's largest lifestyle sports festival (www.surffestival.com). August: British surfing championships in Newquay (www.surfnewquay.co.uk/events.shtml).

 Ten per cent reduction on massage and treatments.

Get a room! Check availability and make reservations through www.mrandmrssmith.com.

The Lugger Hotel Portloe, Truro, Cornwall (01872 501322)
office@luggerhotel.co.uk; www.luggerhotel.co.uk

Le Manoir aux Quat' Saisons

M T W T F ■ M T W T F S S M T W T F S S M T W T F S S M T W T F S S M

Style Gourmet grandeur
Setting Classic Chilterns manor

Great Milton

TFSSMTWTFSSMTWTFSSMTWTFSSMTWTFSSMTWTFSS

raymond blanc's mission
[accomplished] is to
deliver the absolute best
in cuisine and service

Once we'd hit the open (sort of) road after a slow crawl westwards on the A40, we got so carried away we completely missed the turn-off for Great Milton at junction seven. Luckily, as we looked about us in the hotel carpark a little while later, looking faintly ruffled and wondering where the Manoir could be, an extremely helpful man appeared, greeted us and took the car keys. We achieved instant calm as we stepped through an opening in a hedge and heard the expensive whirring of a helicopter coming in to land. We had arrived.

The Manoir is the biggest and oldest house in a very small, very quiet village, and sits regally among beautiful lawns, walled 17th-century and Japanese ponds, and its own extensive herb and organic vegetable gardens, which are heavily featured on the menu (this makes you want to sprawl as you stroll, and eat everything in sight). If the weather had been kinder, we could have played English croquet or French boules, or gone on a picnic made with food fresh from Raymond Blanc's kitchen. As it was, we were content to take it all in, doing our utmost to imagine this was the beginning of a beautiful love affair rather than a one-night fling.

Blanc's mission (accomplished) is to deliver the absolute best in cuisine and service in a friendly atmosphere – he certainly chose the right raw materials in Le Manoir. The old hotel's character is something like a cross between Diana Rigg in an episode of *The Avengers*, and Margaret Rutherford as a 1950s Miss Marple (both in black and white). You feel

For your shoes & Newspapers

caught in a lovely time-warp, with nothing on your mind but fine dining. This, as anyone who has been there will happily tell you, is the whole point; the hotel and its staff are there to create a backdrop for the food, to cocoon you, relax you and accommodate you in gastronomic heaven.

By the time we'd been shown round, our bags had arrived at our room. Called Rouge et Noir, it was quite unexpected and nothing at all like the rest of the hotel: it's an oriental extravaganza, in opium-den style (though not to be confused with the Opium Suite, which is just as sexy). The enormous bed and deeply comfortable cushions soon had us sunk into a much needed sleep. We woke with a start – the room is a bit of a surprise when you don't know where you are – and raced to the lounge just in time for a cream tea. If this sounds like

After a second wander round the gardens as the afternoon turned to evening, it was time for a steaming hot bath and a glass of fine Madeira from the bedside decanter. Then, on with our fine clothes (it seems only right to make an effort to look beautiful when everything around you is such perfection), and to the intimate champagne bar, where we had a glass or two as we pored over the menu and the wine list. The cocktails looked delicious, but we were getting wiser as to pacing ourselves. We weren't the only ones to have dressed up, we noticed. Many people go to the Manoir for a (very) special occasion; for everyone else, being there is worth celebrating in itself. Our fellow guests included a dashing couple in their seventies, an Iranian family with their two children, having a wonderful time, and a mysterious young trio wearing, between them, cowboy boots, a miniskirt and pinstripes.

Earlier on we had looked over the different dining rooms and chosen the conservatory for its clean simplicity and views over the gardens; the inner dining room felt a little formal for us. We sat down among the fresh flowers and white table linen, thrilled that the anticipation was at an end. But first, the wine: the breadth and variety of the list is amazing (some of the prices are, too). Our sommelier was pretty strict-looking, but she was extremely helpful with suggestions. When the gourmet goods arrived, every single taste was perfectly fantastic, and the two half bottles we had chosen were ideal with the menu. Just to give an idea, a sample mènu gourmand at Le Manoir would include ballotine of foie gras with soused cherries and spiced duck; quail egg, spinach, Parmesan and truffle ravioli; roasted best end of new-season Somerset lamb and pan-fried sweetbreads on a sweet garlic purée; hot chocolate fondant, pistachio ice-cream and Amaretto sauce.

It was late when we headed slowly to the drawing room, to sit by the open fire for a few rounds of Scrabble (not too hotly contested) before bed. In the morning, breakfast came exactly as ordered: hot, fresh and very tasty, served in the room's own private fairy-grotto garden.

As we left the Manoir behind, feeling like a king and queen, we realised that even though there's plenty to see nearby; we hadn't once strayed from the hotel and grounds. The simple reason for this is that Le Manoir demands your full attention in order that you properly savour the full gastronomic impact. A trip there is heaven, but not the stuff of whim: save up for a month, and don't eat for a week before you go. We can't all arrive by helicopter, but we can all leave on cloud nine.

Reviewed by Tracey Boyd

Need to know

Rooms 32, each individually designed.

Rates £295–£1,250 (for the two-bedroom suite), including breakfast.

Check-out 11.30am (any later depends on availability).

Facilities Helipad, croquet lawn, bikes, 26 acres of grounds.

Kids Actively welcomed. An extra bed is provided for £45 (not available in deluxe or standard rooms). There is a special menu, and a day's cooking course for children, La Petite Ecole de Cuisine. Babysitting, listening and nanny service available by prior arrangement.

Also Kennels for pets.

In the know

Recommended rooms Among the many contemporary rooms, we preferred the courtyard rooms. Provence and Opium have private terraces. Rouge et Noir is sultry and atmospheric. The Dovecote is very romantic, private and split-level. Anais is very romantic.

Packing tips Loose-fitting trousers/skirt.

Also De-stress in the Japanese Tea Garden.

Food & drink

In the hotel With two Michelin stars, the food is as spectacular as you might expect: try the seven-course menu gourmand.

Dress code Très élégant.

Top table By the windows overlooking the garden. For lunch, in the conservatory.

Last orders Dinner: 9.45pm; 9.30pm for the menu gourmand. Bar: open all night.

Room service 24 hours.

Breakfast 7.30am–10am.

Local restaurants The **Leatherne Bottel** in Goring (01491 872667) serves fantastic food on the river. In Oxford: **Gee's** (01865 553540) for Mediterranean cuisine. **Branca** (01865 556111) for Italian food. The original **Brown's** (01865 511995) for Sunday lunch. **Le Petit Blanc** (01865 510999) serves Modern French brasserie food

Local bars In Oxford: the bar at the **Old Bank Hotel** (01865 799599) on the main street gets lively. **Freud's** (01865 311171) is in a converted church and has live music at weekends.

Local pubs The **Bull** (01844 279726) for a pint. In Oxford: the **Turf** (01865 243235), a trad pub on a cobbled backstreet, for mulled wine on a winter evening. The **Perch** (01865 728891) is by the river.

Worth getting out of bed for

Le Manoir's Ecole de Cuisine is the only school in the world where you can watch and learn in a two-Michelin-star kitchen. Shooting, horse-riding, fishing and golf can also be arranged by the hotel, as can a chauffeur for a trip to Blenheim Palace or Warwick Castle.

Diary June: Henley Royal Regatta (01491 572153; www.hrr.co.uk). July: Garsington Opera at Garsington Manor (01865 361636; www.garsingtonopera.org).

Smith A signed copy of Raymond Blanc's *Foolproof French Cookery*.

Le Manoir aux Quat' Saisons Church Road, Great Milton, Oxford (01844 278881)
lemanoir@blanc.co.uk; www.manoir.com

'Brevity
is the
soul of
lingerie,

'Brevity
is the
soul of
lingerie'

Dorothy Parker

The Onion Store

MTWTFSSMTWTSSMTWTFSSMTWTFS

Style Rustic romance
Setting Leafy New Forest borders

Romsey

TWTFSSMTWTF

A few miles from our destination a thud comes from underneath the car's floor. Despite my untrained ear I recognise this as my exhaust parting company with the rest of my well-travelled vehicle. I realise now that it might not have been the best idea to leave my mobile phone behind in an attempt to get away from it all. But within half an hour we're on our way again with a shiny new exhaust – God bless the mechanics of Totton.

Not far away from the leafy haven of the New Forest, I consult the brochure once again. 'The most intensely private, totally peaceful romantic hideaway,' the hotel proudly declares. It conjures up an image of English rose Jane Seymour, her flowing locks tumbling down onto her white lace dress, looking to camera and saying: 'Some people say romance is back, but I say it never went away.' No, the new exhaust hasn't been leaking fumes, I'm just having a flashback to the Max Factor ad she did in the Eighties.

The Onion Store is wonderfully secluded: four miles out of Romsey, down a series of country lanes. On our arrival a young lady gives us a warm welcome and the promise of tranquillity away from telephones, radio and television. No *Corrie*? No *'Enders*? As our genial host Julia leads us up the garden path to one of only three buildings, set in eight acres of grounds, we contemplate a weekend without any telly. What will we do? Once inside the Grain Store, we glimpse the rustic decor, canopied bed and French cast-iron bath, and our soap-opera withdrawal symptoms vanish clean away. Draped muslin, a tree-trunk balustrade and a pot pourri heart are enough to put even Ann Widdecombe in the mood for a little romance. A quick look at the comments in the guestbook and we're left in no doubt that this place was built for one thing: love.

The next object of our guided tour's attentions is the swimming pool, next to the 17th-century thatched house. Our host Julia had explained we could enjoy late-night candlelit swims, 'Ah... swingers!' my partner jokes. However, we're reliably informed that it's always private and never shared with the other couples. Our guided walk-around complete, we take Julia up on an offer to book us a table at one of the local restaurants, and with a cheery wave she's off, leaving us to our own devices.

My other half decides to test the bath out and, this time, it's John Wayne my mind's eye is seeing. It's a scene from *The Sons of Katie Elder*: the cowboy's in the bath in the middle of the living room, with his family going about their business oblivious to his ablutions – unlike me, who is getting cheeky splashes. Before things develop into a full-scale waterfight, I remind him our tapas meal is beckoning. The Spanish eatery Casa Bodega is only a short journey away and we order the mouth-watering gambas – the perfect finger food to complement this romantic hotel experience.

Back at our woodland retreat, we discover that a rose
has been left on the pillows of our turned-down bed.
The room teeming with Cupid's work, we call it a night.

Overlooking the lingering garlic from our meal the evening
before, breakfast couldn't be more romantic and is
provided in our own secluded spot by the swimming pool.

It's a fresh-fruit platter, followed by a full English breakfast,
delivered with a toast basket in the shape of a little
lamb. With the sun heating up, we are grateful for an
early start and head off to enjoy the countryside.

The New Forest is a haven for walkers and cyclists. Sadly,
for us motorists it is not so heavenly – every time we
reach a town, a traffic jam ensues. One enterprising
hotel in Lyndhurst has turned this to its advantage by
suggesting motorists pull out of the traffic to enjoy a
spot of light refreshment, but we brave it a little further
and reach Lymington, a quaint town on the Solent.
A gently sloping high street leads down to a cobbled
quayside where we stop off at the Ship Inn for a pint.
Feeling more relaxed than we have done in ages, we
raise a toast to the Onion Store. As delighted as
we had been at the handiwork of the Totton mechanics
that got us to our idyllic hideaway, we secretly wish for
a more major motoring breakdown back at the Onion
Store – one that would let us stay a little longer…

Reviewed by Phil Gould

Need to know

Rooms Three converted buildings: the Onion Store, the Grain Store and the Apple Store.
Rates £125–£140, including breakfast.
Check-out 11am. Check-in from 4.30pm.
Facilities Indoor swimming pool, candlelit by night.
Kids The Onion Store is exclusively for couples, so leave the children at home.
Also You may smoke in your private garden. No TV. Open May–October only.

In the know

Recommended rooms Each is superb, with private garden or sundeck.
The Apple Store has its own outdoor hot tub.
Packing tips The premises are unlicensed, so bring your own 'minibar' (ice is supplied).
Books and games provided.
Also Only open May–October; book well in advance. The Onion Store has a sister hotel
in Grenada called Petit Bacaye, a perfect Caribbean hideaway with five palm-thatched
houses on the beach (www.petitbacaye.com).

Food & drink

In the hotel An excellent breakfast is served by the pool. No restaurant.
Local restaurants The **Chesil Rectory Restaurant** in Winchester (01962 851555) is
worth the drive for lunch or dinner. **Casa Bodega** in Romsey (01794 519515) serves
delicious tapas and offers special prices to Onion Store guests. The **George Hotel**
(01983 760331), in Yarmouth on the Isle of Wight, has an idyllic terrace.
Local pubs The **Three Tuns** in Romsey (01794 512639) is a traditional pub with Modern
British food. In Winchester, the **Wykeham Arms** (01962 853834) does good pub food.

Worth getting out of bed for

Get picked up from the Onion Store for an outing in a vintage car (01794 522993).
Have a flying lesson at the Old Sarum Flying Club (01722 322525) or go sailing at
Lymington Town Sailing Club (01590 674514; www.ltsc.co.uk). There's horse-riding in
Brympton (01794 884386). A ferry to the Isle of Wight (www.iwight.com) takes about
half an hour. With its free-roaming ponies, the New Forest itself is wonderful to wander
through (www.thenewforest.co.uk).
Diary July: watch the Admiral's Cup in the Solent (020 7493 2248; www.rorc.org) from
the terrace of the George Hotel. August: Cowes Week on the Isle of Wight (01983
295744; www.cowesweek.co.uk).

Smith A complimentary bottle of Grenadian Rum

Get a room! Check availability and make reservations through www.mrandmrssmith.com.

The Onion Store Romsey, Hampshire (01794 323227)
www.theonionstore.co.uk

The Portobello Hotel

MTWTFSSMTWTF ■ MTWTFSSMTWTFSSMTWTFSSMTW

Style Going boho down in Portobello
Setting Leafy west London

we couldn't believe there could be such peace and quiet in london

For a pair of natural-born South Londoners like our good selves, a sleepover in leafy Notting Hill was an exotic proposition from the start. We've stayed in some beautiful places around the world, but a night 'away' in our home town felt like a nicely naughty novelty. Once we'd called to reserve our room ('the sexy one with the infamous round bed, please') we decided to make no further plans: we didn't tell anyone where we were going, and it wasn't as though we'd be wanting to do all that much in the way of sightseeing. Instant gratification has always appealed to me and, within 45 minutes of leaving home, we're climbing the steps to the Portobello Hotel.

Now, I thought I knew Notting Hill, but I've never set foot on this street before. We're surely talking one of the most covetable corners of the capital; it's all so leafy and calm, I don't miss Brixton at all. The hotel isn't hard to find although there's nothing to distinguish the Portobello from the other discreet and well-kept façades. We'd heard quite a lot about its rock 'n' roll pedigree but didn't know what to expect – certainly not such an undesignery, unpretentious den. My first thought is that we've stumbled into a Belle Epoque bordello: the plants and prints might suggest Victorian gentility, but the scarlet drapes and atmosphere of unshockable discretion whisper 'bring on the dancing girls'.

There are 24 rooms between the basement and the third floor. The Superior rooms, which are the only ones to go for, include the hippie-chic Colonial Room, with its grotto-like basement terrace; the Japanese Room, which also has a small patio; Room 13, with a towering four-poster; and our choice, the Round Bed Room. We shuffle in past the bellboy, shut the door and just smile as we fling ourselves aboard. The bed is in the middle of the room, feet away from an antique bath standing proud between walls decked out in gold-painted bamboo and mirrors. Its enormous showerhead has all sorts of strange and wonderful taps to play with, and I recommend actually using it, rather than just admiring it.

The Bang & Olufsen sound system more than passes muster for mood-setting, and we order a spot of room service before ensconcing ourselves for a couple of hours.

You can see why regular clients at the Portobello include film directors, actors and model agencies: there's character in these here walls (if only

they could speak), and it feels completely private and refreshingly uncommercial. Since there is only a small bar and restaurant within the hotel, we venture out for the evening. Guests get a ten per cent discount at Julie's (also owned by the Portobello), a short walk away; we're loving the louche boho vibe so far, so we decide to stay in the fold.

Julie's warren of rooms feels as intimate and old-school as the Portobello but, unlike the quiet corridors of the hotel, it's buzzing with people, mainly couples. It is supremely romantic; we couldn't have had a nicer evening together. Both of us are in jeans – not a problem in posh-hippie W11, it seems.

It's mid-morning by the time we want breakfast in our round bed. We sit happily picking at croissants, looking out onto the gardens behind the hotel, and remember where we are. Inside the hotel, you could be anywhere, but we're not far from one of the centres of the shopping universe. We spend the rest of the afternoon wandering around Portobello Market, idly thinking about which of the paintings and quirky antiques we might take home. Mrs Smith insists on pilgrimages to girlie magnets the Cross, Aimé and Paul & Joe, and I get a look-in at Nick Ashley, for rough, tough performance wear, and APC. The Paul Smith house on Kensington Park Road is fun for the sheer eye candy on display.

It was a revelation to roam as though we were on holiday, rather than the usual London thing of turning up somewhere only to rush off across town again. We didn't head home for hours, still under a bit of a dreamy spell cast by our out-of-time lovenest. Would we ever cross its threshold again? The Portobello doesn't let you go that easily; I have filed it firmly under 'future spontaneous gestures'. If you're after a certain kind of olden-days charm, it's the only place in town. Put it this way: if Proust had directed erotic films, it would have been on his speed dial.

Reviewed by Felix Buxton

Need to know

Rooms 24: 12 special rooms, six standard doubles, six singles.

Rates £170–£285 for a double room, including continental breakfast.

Check-out About midday, but flexible, in keeping with the relaxed attitude of the hotel.

Facilities Health club, with pool, gym, steam room and massage, a five-minute walk away, £25 a day.

Kids Babysitters by prior arrangement.

In the know

Recommended rooms Room 16, featuring the circular bed, is where Johnny Depp and Kate Moss are said to have filled the Victorian bath with champagne. Room 13 has a four-poster bed with steps leading up to it. Room 1 is the Japanese Room with shell-mosaic patio. Room 2 is the Colonial Room.

Packing tips Dark glasses for people-watching. A varied wardrobe: you never know where you'll end up.

Also Book restaurants well in advance.

Food & drink

In the hotel There is a tiny restaurant/bar with a basic menu. Julie's (owned by the Portobello) is on Portland Road, a ten-minute walk away. Alternatively, Julie's will deliver to your room.

Dress code Laidback rock chic, or whatever you're comfortable in.

Top table Any table in the garden room at Julie's.

Last orders 11pm at Julie's.

Room service Bar and basic menu 24 hours a day.

Breakfast English breakfast available at all hours.

Local restaurants The brasserie at the **Electric** on Portobello Road (020 7908 9696). The hotel can get you a table at **E&O** on Blenheim Crescent for Japanese (020 7229 5454). **Tom's** on Westbourne Grove (020 7221 8818) is good for breakfast, lunch and tea. **Osteria Basilico** on Kensington Park Road (020 7727 9372) is a popular Italian. Have a look at www.gordonramsay.com to see if any of his restaurants take your fancy. **Galicia** (020 8969 3539) has basic decor but great tapas.

Local bars Hotel guests get temporary membership to the **Cobden Club** (020 8960 4222). **Under the Westway** (020 7575 3123) and **Beach Blanket Babylon** (020 7229 2907) are within walking distance.

Local pubs The **Cow** on Westbourne Grove (020 7221 0021) for a pint of prawns. **Golborne House** (020 8960 6260) on Golborne Road for a Mediterranean flavour.

Worth getting out of bed for

For anything from artichokes to antiques, Portobello Market on Saturdays takes over the whole of the Portobello Road. Ice-skating on Queensway (020 7229 0172). The Sportsman Casino in Marble Arch (020 7414 0061) is perhaps not the swankiest of casinos, but membership is free – which is very rare – and it has a very late licence (owing to English law you have to become a member 24 hours before doing any gambling, so plan ahead). The Myla shop on Lonsdale Road (020 7221 9222 www.myla.com) for lingerie and sex toys. Serpentine Gallery (020 7402 6075; www.serpentinegallery.org).

Diary August bank holiday: Notting Hill Carnival. October–November: London Film Festival (www.rlff.com).

Smith 15 per cent off your bill at Julie's, Portland Road – please mention Smithcard on booking your table.

Get a room! Check availability and make reservations through www.mrandmrssmith.com.

The Portobello Hotel 22 Stanley Gardens, London W11 (020 7727 2777)
info@portobello-hotel.co.uk; www.portobello-hotel.co.uk

The Royal Crescent Hotel

MTWTFSSMTWTF◼MTWTFSSMTWTFSSMTWTFSSM Bath

Style Georgian perfection
Setting Atmospheric Bath

subdued and calm
and very, very relaxing

FSSMTWTFSSMTWTFSSMTWTF

I have visited hydrotherapeutic hot spots around the world, including French health resorts, Tunisian hammams and the oldest spa hotel in Hungary. And I am no first-time visitor to Bath; in fact, I have strolled its graceful streets on many an occasion. However, I have never before put two and two together and 'taken the waters'. If you know Bath at all, and have ever walked along the Royal Crescent, you'll know how the perfect proportions of the neo-classical architecture, the cobblestones underfoot and the views of the hills and honey-coloured city epitomise English elegance. The hotel, which occupies the centre of the crescent, is beautiful. As we come to a halt, feasting our eyes, a liveried doorman bids us welcome and takes the car off our hands; we enter what could easily be a very grand private dwelling.

We step into the chequerboard marble-floored hallway, watched by a stately bust of William Pitt the Younger, and, having done the necessary, follow a member of staff to our room. It is classical in decor, and as comfortable as can be. One flop onto our huge bed tells us that the Do Not Disturb sign is going to be put to frequent use; it is large and plump, and envelops us in a sense of luxury. But, as much time as I'd like to spend in bed with my husband, we aren't here to cocoon ourselves away; both the city and the Royal Crescent have much to offer, not least on the bathing front. So it is with a happy sense of expectation that we leave our room and head for the Bath House, which we find within gardens at the back of the hotel.

It is the most perfect small-scale spa: subdued and calm – and very, very relaxing, with treatment rooms, sauna, steam rooms and a pool that is one of the most elegant I have ever seen. It is a far cry from the stale, pale pools in business hotels where pasty execs do lengths in skimpy skivvies. We enter through a large wooden door; gothic windows allow natural light onto the 12-metre pool. Our tired limbs are more than ready to slide into the delicious waters but, before they do, the first of a couple of logistical problems rears its tiresome head. We were unaware that under-12s cannot take a dip, even if they've been training for the Olympics since the age of six months, so we have one very confused three-year-old on our hands. Before our

daughter's thwarted anticipation dissolves into tears, my husband saves the day, whisking her away to the nearby Victoria Gardens where, we are told, there is an extensive children's play area. My second tricky moment of the day is harder to resolve. Do book treatments well before you make your way to Bath. I'm afraid not having a treatment causes me almost enough stress to need one.

A few hours in the tranquil oasis of the Bath House, where I wander in a trance between steam room and plunge pool, losing all track of time, and these disappointments swim away into the realm of the minor hiccup. By the time I'm reunited with husband and daughter, there are smiles all round. I like the thought that I'm following in the tradition of Bath's Georgian heyday, when the fashionable elite came down here to kick back, if that is not too anachronistic a thought. Were we staying just a little longer, I could see myself settling down among the paintings in the library or the drawing room to write archly witty letters dissecting modern society and etiquette...

At six o'clock, we join six other guests, on the hotel's own Twenties river launch, the Lady Sophina. Feeling dozy after my afternoon in the Bath House, I am more than happy to sip champagne and watch the sunny banks of the Kennet and Avon waterway go by. When we get back, we put our tired little one to bed and head to the bar in the Dower House building (the hotel is spread between a number of period houses). In summer, it opens out onto a formal garden area. For swanky metropolitan types who like their cocktails, the wines, beers and spirits on offer might be a slight let-down, but by this time we were feeling so steeped in the Jane Austen feel of our surroundings that a caipirinha wouldn't have scored in the 'right place, right time' stakes.

The hotel's babysitting service giving us our freedom, we dine à deux in the hotel's restaurant, Pimpernel's, with soft lighting and views over the gardens. Loving every minute of our evening together away from the hurly burly, we order an à la carte banquet. Every simple, attractive dish is perfect, and by the time our cherry soufflé with vanilla-bean ice-cream arrives, we have decided that Bath is the new Paris. The Royal Crescent has given us slow-paced luxury, serious service and memorably romantic surroundings. Between these old-school charms and the Bath House, it knocks my list of international hot-springs experiences into a hot tub.

Reviewed by Jori White

Need to know

Rooms 45, including 14 suites.
Rates £220–£850.
Check-out Midday.
Facilities Spa with pool, gym and studio; the hotel's 1920s riverlaunch is available for private charter or champagne cruises; hot-air balloon; an acre of grounds; croquet lawn.
Kids Welcome, although under-12s not permitted in the Bath House.
Also Chauffeur and butler service available.

In the know

Recommended rooms The Master Suite has a vast drawing room and wood-burning fireplace. The rooms at the front have crescent views, those at the back have garden views.
Packing tips Swimwear.
Also Book spa treatments, hot-air-balloon rides and river cruises in advance.

Food & drink

In the hotel Pimpernel's has a Modern European menu.
Dress code Comfortable, but not too comfortable.
Top table A table in the garden, weather permitting.
Last orders Restaurant: 9.45pm.
Room service 24 hours; reduced menu available.
Breakfast 7.30am–10am; Sundays until 10.30am.
Local restaurants The **Fish Works** (01225 448707) on Green Street offers fish-lovers unbeatable freshness and variety. The **Moon and Sixpence Wine Bar and Restaurant** (01225 460962) serves Modern International. **Papillon** (01225 310064) across from the hotel, has great French food.
Local bars **Grappa** (01225 448890) for a pre-dinner cocktail.
Local pubs The **George Inn** in Bathampton (01225 425079) is a tranquil spot by the canal, and another **George Inn** at Norton St Philip (01373 834224) provides fine dining in one of the oldest pubs in the country.

Worth getting out of bed for

Bath Racecourse, Lansdown (01225 424609). Pulteney Bridge: one of only three bridges lined with shops in the world. Roman Baths & Pump Room Royal features natural hot springs (www.romanbaths.co.uk). The Theatre Royal (01225 448844; www.theatreroyal.org.uk).
Diary March: Bath Literary Festival (01225 463362; www.bathlitfest.org.uk). May: Badminton Horse Trials (01454 218272; www.badminton-horse.co.uk). May–June: Bath International Music Festival (01225 463362; www.bathmusicfest.org.uk) features classical, jazz and world music. Early August: Glastonbury Classical Festival (01458 832020; www.glastonburyfestivals.co.uk/classical). Annual horse trials at Gatcombe Park (01937 541811; www.gatcombe-horse.co.uk).

Smith A spa gift from the Bath House

Get a room! Check availability and make reservations through www.mrandmrssmith.com.

The Royal Crescent Hotel 16 Royal Crescent, Bath (01225 823333)
info@royalcrescent.co.uk; www.royalcrescent.co.uk

How to...

...fly a kite

Know your wind: about 5–25mph is ideal for kiting – that's when leaves and crops move gently and constantly, but before it gets really gusty. Choose a common-sense area, away from roads, power lines and airports. Open fields, parks and beaches are just right; the more room you have, the better, of course. Follow the instructions on your kite – and never attempt to fly anything bigger than your own body without help from a friend.

Single-line kites

Stand with your back to the wind. Hold your kite up as high as you can and let it go, feeding the line out. If the wind catches it, the kite will rise; let it, then pull in on the line, and it should climb. Repeat this until your kite reaches the altitude necessary to find a steady wind. If it sinks tailfirst, there might not be enough wind; if it comes down headfirst or spins, there might be too much wind.

Sport kites

With giant sky-duvets and whirly stunt kites, you need to be even more aware of safety, and of potential obstacles to your kiting pleasure. To begin, lay out the kite and lines carefully before you launch. Check all connections; unsnarl and straighten lines and tails. Be sure your flying lines are even, or your kite will spin in one direction as though you were pulling. To launch the kite, step backwards and pull the handles to your sides. Have a friend hold the kite up and launch it into the air, according to wind conditions. Once you are up and away, practice will make perfect: pull the left line to make the kite turn left; pull the right line to turn right. If you're standing still, you're not having enough fun. While you are honing your skills, keep the kite downwind; the further to the side of the wind it flies, the less lift and speed it will have.

The Royal Oak

MTWTF ■ MTWTFSSMTWTFSSMTWT

Style Modernist country comfort
Setting Rural West Sussex

East Lavant

MTWTFSSMTWTFSSMTWTFSSMT

this is the sense of escape we'd had our hearts set on

Spring is here, it's a Friday evening, and all we ask is to get away from the city for the weekend, with no more than an hour in transit, reaching a typically picturesque English village by dusk. Well – you asks, you gets. Night is falling when we arrive in the West Sussex village of East Lavant, and the warm glow of light from the Royal Oak's windows are just the beacon we've been hoping for. From the outside it looks the very image of a quaint old pub; venturing within, we find the cosy atmosphere we were hoping for, but also a modern feel that you don't come across in the average countryside local.

There's a lively bustle and hum, yet it all feels extremely relaxed. The staff give us a warm and friendly reception, and we're accompanied from the main building to our room. Standing at the back of the pub among other outbuildings, it's an entire cottage, complete with its own sitting room, furnished with leather sofas and a plasma-screen TV. Stairs lead to the bedroom, where a very inviting bed awaits us, plus a bathroom with a surprisingly slick walk-in shower. It is a delight to discover that the Royal Oak's design ethic, which unites contemporary style with rustic comfort, applies throughout.

Extremely pleased with our little house, we hotfoot it back to the pub for dinner. (Seeing that there isn't a seat unfilled, we're glad we booked in advance.) The furniture is a mixture: there are a few big oak tables, but we're seated at a curved leather mini sofa; it's all far from rough and rural. There's a wide selection of French wines prominently visible, so we order a bottle while we think about food. The specials board features not only the traditional English comfort fare you'd expect in a village pub, but also a number of dishes with the kind of contemporary flavours – beetroot risotto; monkfish and scallop kebabs – you'd find in a top-drawer metropolitan gastropub. Best of all, the Royal Oak passes our pudding test. We believe any restaurant worth its salt – or sugar and eggs, in this case – must have crème brulée on the menu. The creamy delight in question is creamy and delightful, and we devour it happily, glad to be able to commend our destination honestly.

Opening our curtains the next morning, we're greeted by a beautiful sunny day, so we have our breakfast outside in the courtyard area, under a cloudless sky. During the day it feels less like being in a pub – more like a relaxed hotel. The staff are fully clued up about the area, and tell us about the best walks and what to look out for. Our quarters look even more idyllic in the morning sun; we nip back inside for a brief faff but we're on a mission to see the village by day.

As we come out, we notice some steps to the side of our cottage, leading to a small gate, and then on to what appears to be a boundless sea of tall, swaying corn. Used to streets and walls, we are easily pleased and just stand taking it in. This is the sense of escape we'd had our hearts set on. The stillness is only interrupted by two little children wandering through the field, and a vintage plane humming past overhead.

The village of East Lavant is tiny, with more footpaths than road, and no shops. But who needs 'em when you've got a pretty church and a cricket green? We take a walk up Chalkpit Lane to a viewpoint, where we see how the land lies, looking out over Goodwood and Chichester, with its cathedral and harbour. Glimpsing the sea is too much for us; we just have to get closer. Bosham harbour is only a 20-minute drive from the Royal Oak, and it's classic south coast, full of sailing boats and yachty types. We have a pint at the Anchor Bleu pub, watching the world – OK, dinghies and windsurfers – go by from the terrace. One word of warning: the tide comes in where we parked, and we were told that many drivers have come back to find their cars written off by four feet of water.

Later on, as we dine by the log fire, in the same open-plan room (again, absolutely buzzing), we realise that the accumulation of tiredness we brought with us on Friday has vanished without us even noticing. It took us no longer to get to the Royal Oak from the capital, than it does to get from one side of most cities to the other, but we're miles from the rat race, getting a fix of total tranquillity, and spending a little quality time with nature and with each other. With the style, service and quality of a city hotel, plus the friendliness and charm of the lovely Sussex countryside, this place is a real find.

Reviewed by Mr & Mrs Smith

Need to know

Rooms Six: three behind the pub; three in the main house.
Rates £90–£150.
Check-out Midday.
Kids The split-level Flint Cottage has a sofabed downstairs for children.
Also No smoking in the rooms.

In the know

Recommended rooms Flint Cottage has a 32-inch plasma screen with DVD player.
Room 5 is the largest room in the main house.
Packing tips Binoculars for a day at the races.

Food & drink

In the hotel Excellent pub food in stylish, traditional surroundings.
Dress code Easy chic.
Top table Table 4, in the corner by the fire. Outside in the summer.
Last orders Food stops at 9pm, but you can carry on drinking if you've eaten.
Room service None – ask for a bottle and an ice bucket before last orders.
Breakfast 7am–10am.
Local restaurants The **White Horse** in Chilgrove (01243 535219) does superb
seasonal specialities.
Local bars **Purchases Wine Bar** (01243 537352) is the oldest wine merchants in Chichester.
Local pubs The **Fox Goes Free** in Charlton (01243 811461) does a mean steak and kidney pie,
and real ales. The **Three Horseshoes** in Elsted (01730 825746) is worth the half-hour drive for
the garden with stunning views over the South Downs. **The Anchor Bleu** (01243 573956)
in picturesque Bosham.

Worth getting out of bed for

At Goodwood House (www.goodwood.co.uk) you can have lessons at the Flying Club, go to the
races or watch the racing. While you're there, walk up Trundle Lane to the amazing Seven Points
Viewpoint. Chichester Festival Theatre (www.cft.org.uk) puts on impressive productions; the
Minerva Theatre (01243 781312), next door, does fringe-type performances. West Wittering is
a beautiful sandy beach from which you can walk around to East Head, even more lovely and
secluded. Go riding at Lavant Stables (01243 530460; www.lavanthousestables.co.uk).
Diary June: Polo British Open Championships (01730 813257; www.cowdraypolo.co.uk).
July: Festival of Speed, Goodwood. Horse-racing at Glorious Goodwood (01243 755055;
www.goodwood.co.uk).

Smith Ten per cent off dinner in the restaurant.

Get a room! Check availability and make reservations through www.mrandmrssmith.com.

The Royal Oak Pook Lane, East Lavant, near Chichester, West Sussex (01243 527434)
nickroyaloak@aol.com

we found ourselves in forest as lush
and dense as the malaysian jungle

The Samling

MTWTFSSMTWTF■MTWTFSSMTW

Style **A very English retreat**
Setting **Lakeside wilderness**

Windermere
SMTWTFSSMTWT

right on the water but still secluded

After half a day in the car I got a huge surge of excitement as we approached the lakes. There, nestled in soft undulating hills and perfect woods rolling down to Lake Windermere, is the Samling. You couldn't ask for a more ideal location – right on the water, but still secluded. It's no wonder so many celebrities have chosen to stay to escape to it. As we arrived, Nigel the manager appeared from nowhere like Mr Benn. He showed us to our own ranch-style abode, told us everything we needed to know and then vanished.

We'd booked into Lethera, our own three-storey cottage. At the bottom was a huge bathroom, stocked with candles and Molton Brown goodies; it left a lot to the imagination – in a good way. Next floor up was our chill-out room. A comfy worn-in sofa, telly, sound system and realistic-looking gas fire made it as cosy as can be. But, better than all the mod cons that money can buy, we were astonished by the most incredible view of the lake. At the top was a bed with big fluffy pillows, and, even more fantastic, another chance to get a load of that vista.

Having arranged with Nigel when we wanted to have dinner, we popped down to the main house for an aperitif. Here, in the drawing room, you choose supper from three menus. For those who find navigating their way through the à la carte and tasting menus for vegetarians and carnivores a little challenging, Nigel soon jumps to the rescue. And while he was helping us to choose an excellent bottle of red, some delicious canapés arrived: quail's eggs, duck confit, Iberico ham – even a frog's leg. Just as I was coveting the sofa by the open fire (snapped up by couples who get down there before 8pm), Nigel came to distract us with news of all the activities available. Whether you want to fish, walk or go boating on the lake, Mr Benn can arrange it. I knocked my champagne back and declared that tomorrow we would be learning to fly-fish.

The restaurant was a little more formal than we'd expected, but none of the other couples batted an eyelid at my combats and loud shirt, and it was to the happy clinking sound of a lot of lead crystal that we enjoyed a delicious meal. Full from organic chicken baked in straw, we felt gluttonous thinking of our next meal straight after dinner, but they like you to order breakfast the night before. With the choice of a four-course sit-in or a cup-of-tea wake-up call and your food brought in later, we chose a 9am kick-off in the main house.

Sat at the table by the window, with a fantastic view over the lake once again, we were glad we'd been greedy and requested all that we could. A full English polished off and belts loosened, it was time for a walk. The beauty of the Samling's woodland location is that you can step outside your room and start walking – we soon found ourselves in forest as lush and dense as a Malaysian jungle. We made our way back just in time for our fly-fishing lesson.

We'd never been fishing before, but Patrick Arnold soon had us on the fast track to learning the true art of casting, and after an hour's expert tuition on the bank he let us loose on the lake. Wow! Catching my first fish ever was a real moment. In fact, I've since splashed out on my own rod, and I'm still boring people with the story.

What an ideal escape our Samling stay turned out to be – the chance to recharge our batteries, and an adventure to boot. As we were packing up to leave, I was almost relieved to find a flat tyre on the car, in the hope we'd have to stay another night. But, of course, a resourceful Nigel jumped to the rescue with a portable pump and (somewhat begrudgingly) we were on our way.

Reviewed by Oliver Tress

Need to know

Rooms Ten.
Rates £195–£395, including breakfast.
Check-out 11am.
Facilities Pool table, communal hot tub, 67 acres of grounds.
Kids Kids are welcome, but there are no babysitting facilities.
Also No smoking in the restaurant.

In the know

Recommended rooms We liked the Bothy. Also Manmire, a split-level room away from the main house, with spectacular views. Only one room doesn't have a view of Lake Windermere.
Packing tips Walking shoes, wet-weather gear, CDs; there is a VHS classic-film library.

Food & drink

In the hotel Fine dining, with a fantastic wine cellar.
Dress code Country casuals.
Top table By the window, for a view over the lake.
Last orders 9.30pm for food, but the bar stays open all night for guests.
Room service Until 11pm.
Breakfast 7.30am–10am.
Local restaurants **L'Enclume** in Cartmel (01539 536362; see page 102) for fine dining.
Local pubs The **Drunken Duck** (01539 436347; see page 96) on the opposite side of the lake is great for lunch or dinner. The **Mortal Man** (01539 433193) in Troutbeck serves good pub food and real ales.

Worth getting out of bed for

Croquet on the lawn; horse-riding, fishing, sailing, ballooning and water-skiing can all be arranged by the hotel. If you fancy organising water sports yourself, visit www.lakedistrictletsgo.co.uk for a list of companies in the area. Contact Patrick Arnold at Esthwaite Water (01539 436541) for tuition in fly-fishing.
Diary August: Grasmere Sports and Show for Cumberland Wrestling and fell-running; the Vale of Rydal Sheepdog Trials (01539 432582), including show-jumping for Jack Russells, which has to be seen to be believed.

Smith Free room upgrade, subject to availability.

Get a room! Check availability and make reservations through www.mrandmrssmith.com.

The Samling Ambleside Road, Windermere, Cumbria (01539 431922)
info@thesamling.com; www.thesamling.com

Seaham Hall and Serenity Spa

TFSSMTWTFSSMTWTF MTWTFSSMTWTFSSMTWTFSSM

Style Tip-top technology
Setting Windswept Durham clifftop

the spa has more feng shui
cred than you can shake
a perfectly honed limb at

TFSSMTWTFSSMTWT SSMTWTFSSM TWTFS

Seaham Hall is swathed in history: Lord Byron married Annabella Milbanke at Seaham Hall in 1815, and the ancient stones of Hadrian's Wall are a short drive away. However, this is one hotel that faces resolutely towards the future. As the William Pye water sculpture in front of the clifftop house declares, Seaham and its facilities are as 21st-century as they can be. When we were shown into our suite, we were offered a guided tour – that is, a demonstration of how to use the intelligent lighting, surround-sound ceiling speakers, CD banks, Internet access (with ISDN), outside-temperature indicators, bedside and doorside master controls for adjustable mood lighting, and pinpoint reading lights, complete with sleep mode. Not a promising start for a technophobe like myself, but the boyfriend loved it. That's the modern

bit; traditional comforts include fireplaces throughout, private terraces off the ground-floor suites, and sea views from almost all the rooms. Our bathroom, like our sleeping quarters, was luxuriously spacious, with a romantic two-person bath (candles come as standard). On booking, we had been offered a choice of pillows, and our superking bed more than lived up to such promise. All in all, hours of fun for techno fans and luxury fiends alike.

After a couple of cocktails and a good go mucking about with the gadgets, we pulled ourselves together for dinner. The hotel's restaurant has delicious daily-changing menus. (One woman I met in the sauna the next day told me she and her husband eat here every week because the food is just so good.) Rare wines are available from the cellar, which is open for private tastings, so you can taste wines during the day and pick your favourite to sip while you dine.

Brightish and earlyish the next day, we checked out Seaham Hall's gym (yet more incredibly advanced machines, but there's human help on hand, too), and its breathtaking spa. The spa is built into the hillside, has more feng shui cred than you can shake a perfectly honed limb at, and combines exotic therapies with modern perfectionism. As we entered the underground tunnel that that leads from the hotel to the spa, in towelling robe and flip-flops, we felt as though we'd wandered into a world that revolved around our pleasure and comfort.

The treatments on offer include Japanese facials, Chinese massage and Balinese Milk Ritual wraps; you'll wish you had an entire week to try them all out. Everyone else, including the lucky locals (this is definitely one of the best hotel spas in the UK), feels the same, so be sure to book weekend treatments well in advance. If you haven't seen much of your loved one lately, or you can't get enough of each other, you can learn massage

together or just indulge at the same time in the same treatment room. Downstairs, we found the aromatherapy-based snail shower (so called because of its shape), a 20-metre ozone-cleansed pool, sauna, steam room, ice fountain and hydrotherapy bath. These watery chill-out zones take a good two hours alone; we were feeling weak by noon, and took a break from relaxing to snack on stir-fry and fresh juice in the Thai brasserie.

The plan had been to investigate the quaint historic charms of Durham after lunch, but we felt inspired to get really romantic, and drove east to Corbridge for a walk along Hadrian's Wall. Feeling invigorated (and perhaps a little windswept), we headed north into Newcastle as it got dark, and got a look at the stunning Millennium Bridge (Building of the Year in 2002) at its illuminated best. Newcastle is absolutely buzzing by night, and well deserves its reputation for superfly bars, clubs and restaurants. We were sorry to leave our new favourite region on Sunday, but we'll be back for more. On one hand, Seaham feels remote – remote from the everyday, with its super-deluxe facilities and chintz-free decor (the rooms and suites are impeccably chic, at the luxe end of corporate, with furnishings in elegant chocolates, beiges and greens). On the other hand, it's in easy reach of a revitalised metropolis, with the aforementioned gamut of fleshpots and eating establishments, as well as cultural jewels such as the new Baltic complex at Gateshead. One weekend at this hotel is somehow not quite enough.

Reviewed by Mr & Mrs Smith

Need to know

Rooms 18 suites and a penthouse, most with sea views. Ground-floor suites have private terraces.
Rates From £195; penthouse suite, from £525, including breakfast.
Check-out Midday.
Facilities The Serenity Spa, fully equipped gymnasium.
Kids Welcome in the hotel and restaurant, and at certain times in the Serenity Spa. Babysitting service by prior arrangement.
Also No smoking in restaurant, but permitted in the bar and lounge. Pets not welcome.

In the know

Recommended rooms The Penthouse. Room 11, intimate and south-facing.
Room 14, with balcony overlooking the spa. Room 15, with a bath in the bedroom.
Packing tips A kite, walking boots, swimsuit and goggles for the pool.
Also Flip-flops and dressing gowns are provided.

Food & drink

In the hotel The menu in the restaurant changes daily. Ozone, the Thai brasserie and juice bar, serves fresh wok-cooked dishes, juices and energy drinks all day.
Dress code Spruce up for dinner.
Top table Any table by the window overlooking the terrace.
Last orders Food: 9.30pm. Bar: normal licensing hours.
Room service 24 hours.
Breakfast 7am–10.30am.
Local restaurants In Newcastle: **Treacle Moon**, Quayside (0191 232 5537) has an international menu. **Fisherman's Lodge**, Jesmond Dene (0191 281 3281) is in a contemporary setting and serves excellent modern dishes. **Rooftop Restaurant** at Baltic (0191 440 4949) – book well in advance.
Local bars In Quayside: **Pravda** (0191 261 9001), a Russian-themed vodka bar, and the **Quilted Camel** (0191 221 1880) which has a great vibe at weekends.
Local pubs The **Angel** at Corbridge (01434 632119) for bistro food.

Worth getting out of bed for

Go-karting and quad-biking at Karting North East (0191 521 4050), a five-minute drive away.
Bamburgh Castle (01668 214515) overlooks miles of unspoilt sandy beach. A walk around the most important Roman remains site in Britain, Hadrian's Wall (www.hadrians-wall.org).
Diary January: New Year's Day Dip, Whitley Bay, for the first swim of the year. June: John Smith's Northumberland Plate, the North's answer to Ladies Day at Ascot, Newcastle Race Course (0191 236 2020; www.newcastle-racecourse.co.uk). July: Sunderland International Kite Festival (01923 822085).

Smith Room upgrade, subject to availability, and an Elemis Home Spa Ritual gift.

Get a room! Check availability and make reservations through www.mrandmrssmith.com.

Seaham Hall and Serenity Spa Lord Byron's Walk, Seaham, County Durham (0191 516 1400)
reservations@seaham-hall.com; www.seaham-hall.com

a stroll
through
gently
swaying
fields
gave us
our fix of
rural idyll

The Star Inn

Style *Out of Africa*
meets gastropub
Setting Sleepy North
Yorkshire moors

candlelit
nooks,
padded
pews and
a faint
whiff of
woodsmoke
and
beeswax

It's a known fact that the wives of Yorkshire farmers have a hard time persuading their husbands to go on holiday. Their concerns about the landscape of the proposed destination (will it be as beautiful?), the food (will it be as tasty?), the breakfasts (will they be as big?) and the bed (will it sag in the middle?) are enough to keep them anchored to home. It was with this in mind that we went to find out exactly why it is they'd rather not stray from Yorkshire.

Fine mists swirl all round as we approach the hamlet of Harome, home of the Star Inn. But any *American Werewolf in London* thoughts dissipate with the cheery welcome we receive as we arrive at the Star Inn's 'corner shop'. A Wavy Line it is not; this Aladdin's cave of comestibles would give any traiteur in Lyons a run for his gastronomic money. It's packed with wonderful local and British produce, together with an abundance of delicacies from the Star Inn kitchen. After checking our bags in at the guest-house, our first priority is getting a taste of the Star's edibles for ourselves.

Conveniently, the converted guest-house is just across the road from the 14th-century thatched inn; oak furnishings, ancient low beams, candlelit nooks, padded pews and a faint whiff of woodsmoke and beeswax in the air conjure up 600 years of hospitality. Andrew, one half of the Jacquie and Andrew Pern partnership, is the head chef, whose northern roots inspire his brilliant Michelin-starred menu. Having feasted on slices of beef so perfectly rare they melt in the mouth, we tear ourselves away from the warmth and cosiness of the Inn and head back to the Cross House Lodge.

Stopping off for a quick nightcap from the honesty bar, we ease into the comfy sofas of the residents' lounge to take in our surroundings. Enormous beams, open fires and an incredible dining-room table provide a look that is *Out of Africa* meets Yorkshire barn, with an added dose of modern-day design. Andrew's robust taste in food is matched by Jacquie's taste in decor. Under the watchful gaze of the head of an African wildebeest and a couple of springbok, we retire to our room.

We wake up in heaven. Figs, prosciutto, warm breads, smoked salmon, brioche, yoghurt, muesli, delicious cheeses and caffè latte are all waiting for us at our own little garden table in the sunshine. After a breakfast on cloud nine, this Mr Smith heads for the oak-panelled bathroom, where I have the boyish joy of adding so much bubble bath to the enormous tub that as soon I discover the 'spa' button, the ensuing foam is reminiscent of *espuma* nights in Ibiza. But as I submerge myself in the ginger and ginseng bubbles,

my uplifting soundtrack is Mozart, not Manumission. Meanwhile, Mrs Smith takes a tour of the sheet music on the piano in our room, plays patience with Alice in Wonderland-proportioned playing cards (covering the whole super-kingsize bed) and polishes off a jar full of home-made cookies. Eventually, she trots in and turns the spa bath off, informing me it is already midday.

A stroll past ducklings in the village pond and fields with gently swaying corn gives us our fix of rural idyll, and help us work up an appetite for lunch in the Star's restaurant, also located in the longhouse. We order the pot-roast Duncombe Park partridge (named after a stately home five miles down the road) with Fadmoor beetroot, creamed curly kale and smoked bacon gravy – delicious. The wine list is a delight, too; extensive and unpretentious, it is clearly compiled with diners in mind, rather than to satisfy the ego of an over-ambitious sommelier. Before we leave the Star Inn, we raise a farewell toast to the local farmers' wives and their reluctance to travel very far afield. After this particular Yorkshire sojourn, we understand completely why they would rather stay put.

Reviewed by Mr & Mrs Smith

Need to know

Rooms Eight in Cross House Lodge; three suites in Black Eagle Cottage.

Rates £120–£210.

Checkout Midday, but flexible.

Kids Welcome. There is a play area in the garden.

Also No smoking in the restaurant.

In the know

Recommended rooms Cross House Lodge: Room 1 has a bath at the foot of the bed. Room 5 is large, with its own snooker table. Room 7 has a double bath. Room 8 has a spa bath, private garden and piano. Black Eagle Cottage: the Garden Shed is open-beamed with a private terrace.

Packing tips Take an appetite and a shopping list.

Also Book the restaurant (closed on a Monday) in advance. There's a private dining room in the pub that seats ten. The Wheelhouse dining room in the Cross House Lodge can cater for parties of up to 20 residents.

Food & drink

In the know Michelin-starred British food, featuring spiced-up old favourites.

Dress code Casual smart.

Top table The round table in the corner. In the pub: in the garden or by the fire.

Room service 8am–10pm.

Breakfast 8.30am until late, or a breakfast picnic in your room until 11am.

Local restaurants The **Crab and Lobster** in Asenby (01845 577286) for exquisite seafood. The **Tontine Inn** in Staddlebridge (01609 8826741) does top-notch bistro food.

Local pubs The **Blue Lion** in East Witton (01969 624273) serves great food. The **Appletree Country Inn** in Marton (01751 431457) is a superb gastro. The **Golden Lion** in Osmotherly (01609 883526) is a beamed pub that's good for a pint.

Worth getting out of bed for

Flying lessons at Yorkshire Gliding Club (01845 597237). Pickering Trout Lake (01751 474219). Middleham racehorse-training centre (www.middlehamonline.com). Visit York for shopping and the Minster. A stomp across the Yorkshire Moors. Quad-trekking with the Quad Squad (07715 757706; www.quadbikes.fsnet.co.uk).

Events July: the Great Yorkshire Show (01423 541222; www.greatyorkshireshow.org) for show-jumping, shopping, Pig of the Year; Ryedale Festival for recitals, concerts and opera (01751 475777; www.ryedalefestival.co.uk). August: Castle Howard Proms (08452 256020; www.castlehoward.co.uk).

Smith A complimentary picnic hamper filled with goodies from the Star Inn's kitchen.

Get a room! Check availability and make reservations through www.mrandmrssmith.com.

The Star Inn Harome, near Helmsley, North Yorkshire (01439 770397)
www.thestaratharome.co.uk

Stoke Park Club

Style His 'n' hers luxury leisure
Setting Top-hole Bucks golf course

a stone's throw from where james
bond had a round with goldfinger

Getting to Stoke Park Club is almost disappointingly easy. Mrs Smith is still griping that Mr Smith can't be bothered to take her further out of town than a whisper past the M25, when they're turning off a dull suburban lane onto a tree-lined driveway to the club-house at Stoke Poges. It's an enormous, imposing stately mansion designed by Mad King George III's architect, which if it weren't for the Union Jack flying, would look like a mini White House. As you approach you feel like you've finally 'arrived' – you're aristos, at last.

We park our Mercedes (van) amongst Porsches and Beamers a stone's throw from where James Bond had his famous round of golf with Goldfinger, and climb the same steps to reception Hugh and Renée did for their dirty weekend in *Bridget Jones*. By now we're starting to feel pretty special. Then it's up a grand staircase lit by an impressive chandelier to our Executive King Room.

Our private quarters are traditional and plush, with a huge bed covered in linen-clad pillows, a red velvet sofa at its foot; since we've booked ourselves the Celebration Package, some chocolate-dipped strawberries and a chilled bottle of champagne are awaiting us. Without further ado, we get our kit off… after all, Stoke Park has its own incredible spa, SPA SPC, separate from the mansion, with an inviting indoor pool looking over the gardens through a wall of glass, and a gym with so many exercise contraptions in it your eyes water just looking at them. There are also more tennis courts than you could imagine they'd ever need.

Massaged, pummelled and polished, we return to the room, quaff our champagne, don our glad-rags, and descend the sweeping staircase to dinner. Given the size of the mansion, the main restaurant is surprisingly small, but it's imaginatively decorated, and a helpful waiter settles us into the leopard-print cushions on one of the purple velvet banquettes. Full from a delicious meal of squid, ravioli, steak and sea-bass, and plenty of antipodean chardonnay, it's through the pink velvet sofas and curtain-swathed Orangery (the daytime bar and tea and scones room), and on to the President's Bar. It's a traditional mahogany-panelled sportsmen's bar with endless plaques adorning the walls and the club's champion golfer enshrined in gold leaf for ever more. Unfortunately for the staff, we also find the snooker table in a room all of its own down below, which we have to ourselves until very, very late. Our poor barman is particularly gracious and plies us with as many cognacs, Cobras and Cohibas as we could manage until finally we admit defeat. Staggering back upstairs we find him snoring softly, head in hands.

Waking up from our delicious linen-induced slumber, not only have we missed breakfast but we are also in serious danger of being late for our golf lesson. And our sore heads have a lot of rules to take in: soft spikes, hard spikes, collared shirts (tucked in), tailored culottes for the ladies, for the gents, plus-fours (and we thought you have those with coffee), no denim and definitely no trainers. A sheepish Mr Smith drags his heels to the driving range, attempting to hide his feet.

Our embarrassment at being riff-raff over, we meet our delightful instructor Tim. Rather than making us feel like the golfing muppets we are, he introduces us to the game with charm and enthusiasm. He points down to the end of the range where Algernon, a priceless statue, stands at a (very) safe distance of 300 yards. Once we get to grips with our grip, stance and swing, our aim is to try and hit Algy. Nothing like a childish incentive to get us hooked. We golf straight through until it is time to leave. On settling the bill at the golf shop, Mr Smith declares he's intent on having his name join those on the plaques in the bar, and suggests we go on golfing weekends more often. I'm with him, so long as the plus-fours are Prada, the après-golf lengthy and the backdrop Stoke Park Club.

Reviewed by Mr & Mrs Smith

Need to know

Rooms 21, including three suites.
Rates £280–£1,100.
Check-out 11am.
Facilities Golf; 350 acres of parkland; the SPA SPC with indoor pool, 13 indoor and outdoor tennis courts, gym, dance studio and treatment centre.
Kids Children are welcome: high chairs and babysitters by arrangement.

In the know

Recommended rooms If the budget will stretch, ask for the four-poster suite that Hugh and Renée shared in *Bridget Jones' Diary*. Otherwise, ask for a room with a view.
Packing tips Swimwear; tennis kit, golf clubs.
Also Clear your credit card: golf is not a cheap hobby, and the shop sells everything you may have forgotten or never knew you needed.

Food & drink

In the hotel The Park serves Modern British cuisine, and the best Sunday lunch in the area. The Orangery serves breakfasts, snacks and afternoon tea. The Beach Bar, in the Pavilion, serves healthy snacks and juices.
Dress code No trainers, only smart denim, shirts for the boys.
Top table By the window for the view.
Last orders All restaurants take last orders at 9.30pm and close at 10pm. Drinking goes on as late as you do.
Room service 24-hour full menu.
Breakfast In bed or all day in the Orangery; 7am–10am in the Park restaurant.
Local restaurants The Michelin-starred **Waterside Inn** at Bray (01628 620691).
The Michelin-starred **Fat Duck** (01628 580335).
Local pubs The **Royal Oak** at Farnham Common (01753 642032) is about ten minutes away and does good pub grub.

Worth getting out of bed for

Golf lessons at the hotel by prior arrangement. Also riding lessons and outings at the local equestrian centre. Windsor for everything royal and, of course, the polo.
Diary June: Boodle & Dunthorne Champions Challenge for tennis (020 7384 4877; www.bdcc.info); Royal Ascot (01344 622211; www.ascot.co.uk). July: Cartier International Polo at Windsor (01784 434212; www.guardspoloclub.com).

Smith Room upgrade, subject to availability, and a free bottle of champagne on arrival.

Get a room! Check availability and make reservations through www.mrandmrssmith.com.

Stoke Park Club Park Road, Stoke Poges, Buckinghamshire (01753 717171)
info@stokeparkclub.com; www.stokeparkclub.com

Strattons

everything about the place is worth shouting about

SSMTWTFSSMTWTF■MTWTFSSMTWTFSSMTW

Style Eco-friendly eclectic
Setting The Brecks in Norfolk

Swaffham

Tucked away off the high street of the cute market town of Swaffham, Strattons is a beautiful Queen Anne Palladian villa set in its own close. Chickens roaming the front lawn were the first to greet us, followed by the warmly welcoming owners, Vanessa and Les. Once checked in, we were ushered back out onto the drive and taken across to a converted outhouse set apart from the hotel – our home for the weekend.

An appealing mixture of modern and ethnic decor, and split between two floors, the Opium Suite is so much of a haven even the chooks were determined to cop a look inside. Downstairs is the sitting room, with a walk-in wet room behind glass bricks (first-time-awayers may find themselves waving goodbye to a little of that mystery). As for the bath, we found it standing at the foot of the bed upstairs – fabulously unconventional. If you're planning a detox, this is the retreat for you; everything is as organic and eco-friendly as possible, even the bubble-bath. We had other plans though, and a complimentary bottle of Madeira caught our eye.

After familiarising ourselves with the bar situation (for the rooms without minibars, it's located in a dresser in one of the drawing rooms and is run on an honesty basis) we were ready for a wander through Swaffham before dinner. There, we were treated to an unexpected auction: lots of country folk in wellies, Barbours and flat caps crowded around a hoary old man with hub caps and tools spread out on tarpaulins in front of him – all advertised in that incomprehensible auctioneer patter. There were also some great cheese and fish stalls at the market, which got us in the mood for our supper.

Les and Vanessa really are in their element at dinnertime; she cooks and he's the host. Les serves drinks in one of the two adjoining drawing rooms and takes your order. I had a perfect Kir Royale by the fire and gazed at the unusual art while Les talked us through the wine list. Actually, one of the highlights of our stay was Les on sommelier duty; his enthusiasm was most endearing.

Aperitif down the hatch, we moved into the restaurant, where a mural of an Italian summer country scene, small windows, low ceilings and church candles create a pretty, cosy feel. It is wonderfully intimate, and thus not a place to discuss anything delicate (although after a while we became oblivious – who could resist so many great half bottles of white?) The food is hearty all-organic English fare, served in contemporary style: home foods with a creative twist. Les' talent for description extends to the cheese. He described his favourite variety as having a taste 'reminiscent of corned beef' and I confess I found it hard not to chuckle. In accordance with the hotel's eco conscience, if food is not grown at the hotel (all the eggs come from the chickens we'd met), it's from local farmers and producers. So green-minded is Strattons, its stringent recycling policy has even won several awards.

Meals are always a great time to clock your fellow guests, and though we'd noticed a septuagenarian majority in the sparsely populated town, the hotel's guests were noticeably younger. A young Camilla Parker Bowles-a-like, with pearls, turned-up collar, and hubby resplendent in blazer and tie chatted amicably with a Duffer-clad twentysomething urbanite and his girlfriend.

Dinner was a hard act to follow, but breakfast was just as impressive. Exceptionally tasty eggs, bacon, mushrooms and delicious eco coffee in huge mugs set us up for our drive to the beach (and soothed the consequences of champagne in the bath in our bedroom the night before). And wow, what a beach. Who knew beaches like this existed in our Blighty? Sand-dunes and a long, flat expanse to fly our stunt kite from – it's so massive it feels like no one else is around, apart from the birds. Surrounded by the Holkham Salt Marshes Wildlife Reserve, we saw thousands of Canada geese. When they took off, we stopped and stared: the sky went black and they made a right royal din. Talk about disturbing the peace – at least it wasn't us, for a change. But we couldn't help it at Strattons; the decor, the food, the surroundings – everything about the place is worth shouting about.

Reviewed by Mr & Mrs Smith

Need to know

Rooms Eight.
Rate £100–£200, including breakfast.
Check-out 11.30am.
Kids Welcome. Babysitters can be arranged.
Also Non-smoking throughout.

In the know

Recommended rooms The Opium Suite, tucked away from the main house. The Red Room has private gardens. The Venetian for its incredible walnut kingsize bed. The small but funky Seagull Room.
Packing tips Cool-box, so you can take some of the local produce home with you; slippers for the stone floor in the Opium Suite.
Also Lunch is not available.

Food & drink

In the hotel Delicious and inventive dinners, using the finest local and organic produce in their award-winning restaurant.
Dress code Wholesome, relaxed.
Top table Go for a corner, or a window table in the summer.
Last orders Food: 9pm. Drinks: normal licensing hours.
Room service No, but there is an honesty bar for late-night drinks.
Breakfast Weekdays: 7.30am–10am; weekends 8.30am–10am.
Local restaurants The **Crown Hotel** in the Buttlands, Wells-next-the-Sea (01328 710209) is great for supper. The **Victoria at Holkham** (01328 711008; see page 204) has barbecues in summer.
Local pubs The **Walpole Arms** in Itteringham (01263 587258) is a great gastropub for Sunday lunch. The **Hoste Arms** in Burnham Market (01328 738777) is another gastro option. The **Hare Arms** at Stow Bardolph (01366 382229) is traditional. The **Albert Victor** at Castle Acre (01760 755213) for a pint.

Worth getting out of bed for

The Brecks offers miles of forest, heath and farmland; a couple of minutes from the hotel and you can be on an old road that leads over Swaffham heath where you can walk, jog, cycle or ride. Or why not try tree trekking, tarzan swings and high wires with Go Ape (www.goape.cc) at High Lodge? Visit the antiques market and auction in Swaffham on Saturdays or go for a picnic on the beach. Hire a boat on the Norfolk broads from George Smith & Sons (01603 782527; www.norfolkbroads.com). Karting at North Pickenham (01760 441777; www.anglia-karting.co.uk). Horse-riding at Bridlewood Livery & Riding Centre, Downham Market (01366 385923). Take the car of your dreams for a spin on the Snetterton Racetrack (0870 512 5250).
Diary October: Champion's Day at Newmarket (01638 663482; www.newmarketracecourses.co.uk). November: Open Pit Lane at Snetterton Race Circuit (01953 887303).

Smith A bespoke spa box by Savonnerie.

Get a room! Check availability and make reservations through www.mrandmrssmith.com.

Strattons 4 Ash Close, Swaffham, Norfolk (01760 723845)
enquiries@strattons.co.uk; www.strattonshotel.com

Hotel Tresanton

M T W T F ▪ M T W T S S M T W T F S S M T W T F S S M T W T F S S

Style Miami beach house with a touch of the Med
Setting Chocolate-box Cornish village

log pillows are great for lazy
daytime reads in bad weather or
intriguing evening pursuits

'Sorry, sir, your car still isn't ready.' These are not the words you want to hear the morning you plan to take the lady away for a weekend of fine loving. Unless, like me, you have Germanic blood coupled with a Tourette's-like argumentative disorder: I tend to see these things as opportunities rather than problems. I go red, the garage guy goes apologetic, and 23 minutes later a Porsche Boxter appears. For, as that PJ O'Rourke manqué Jeremy Clarkson will tell you, silly cars are the key to bearable weekending sans PlayStation 2.

Our weekend is to be spent at Hotel Tresanton, the place that began Cornwall's transformation from a two-week bucket-and-spade destination to chic mini-break hotspot. 300 miles of sinuous open road from London and the boutique-hotel reputation gears one (well, me) up to find it annoying before arrival. Did I mention that I argue for sport? But first impressions impress. A Greek-style passage and stone staircase lead to a raised sun deck that is set into the cliff face

and dotted with old steamer chairs that recall *The Talented Mr Ripley*. Sadly, I do not resemble Jude nor my girlfriend Gwyneth. Nonetheless, hazy visions of sun-drenched cocktails help me unwind, and any residual rant evaporates in the face of the hotel's fantastic old porter – a man well worth tipping – who proves a fountain of local knowledge. Realisations that there is no need to talk a) so fast, or b) so much rubbish follow as I slip into gear for the weekend.

The hotel is situated on Cornwall's often overlooked southern coast, between picturesque St Mawes and the rolling fields spliced with public footpaths leading to Falmouth. A former yachting club, Tresanton was built from a cluster of old houses in the Fifties, hence its higgledy-piggledy levels and port-town setting. St Mawes and Tresanton have been a preserve of the sailing set for years, but it is only since the 1999 reopening, after an extensive refurbishment to bring it up to the standard expected by owner Olga Polizzi and her chi-chi A-list clientele that it has achieved its Halkin-on-sea tag.

The decor is posh, eclectic and relaxed. It's also eco-friendly; ash floors, fired-earth tiles, organic paint and local granite work surfaces feature throughout. The laid-back drawing room probably best illustrates Polizzi's grab-bag taste, combining slouchy sofas (ideal for reading, and Tresanton's wicked afternoon teas) with Greek busts, Chinese chequers, a huge log fire, and French windows leading to a sprawling sundeck.

There are 29 rooms in the hotel. Ours was cosy yellow with crisp Egyptian cotton bedlinen, a tasteful seaside feel and log pillows great for lazy daytime reads in bad weather or intriguing evening pursuits. A magnificent harbour view makes me momentarily forget what hit me when I first entered the room... namely, it was small. (My argue-mentor John McEnroe's voice starts ringing through my head. '£250? You cannot be serious!') I twitch for an argument. The girlfriend finds my argumentative disorder an embarrassment; as a release mechanism, I have learned to 'sneak argue' – she doesn't get annoyed, I get my fix. I say something like 'I need to get my cigarettes from the car', then trail off, following the vein pulsing like an anaconda in my forehead, and return 20 minutes later, happy, but unpopular among hotel staff. After this particular episode, I can vouch that Tresanton's staff are more than polite – calming and motherly, even – and that there *are* bigger rooms, only you have to know what you are asking for. Hell, even Tony Blair was recently knocked back owing to a full house. At least I get a room. Z-list paranoia disperses.

The bar, situated on the lower floor, is Tresanton's greatest asset (in no small part because I am an aspiring alcoholic): cute mini armchairs, chocolate and tan pepper Amtico flooring, clotted-cream walls and clever lighting that could make even Dot Cotton look unravaged, nay, sexy. Candles at night light an enchanting trail to the buzzy conservatory restaurant whose Mod Med food is definitely worth sampling. Local pubs are also worth a look. We skipped the more expensive places; a cursory glance at the menus showed that most followed Tresanton's lead rather too faithfully. (We started to wonder whether there are underground tunnels from Olga Polizzi's kitchen.)

As weather was good the following day, we opted to try the Padstow-Bodmin camel trail. Driving there in the PS2 substitute, we found a brisk walk along the path was exertion enough to give us a glow without making us wheeze. Back at the Tresanton for a farewell drink, I fall into a weird half sleep in my girlfriend's arms listening to the sea and dreaming of Grand Theft Auto. Forget eastern mysticism: when my girlfriend, the game and guest-house blurred together, I knew true happiness.

Reviewed by Alex Proud

Need to know

Rooms 29, most with a sea view: nine with a terrace, two family suites.
Rates £165–£400, including breakfast.
Check-out 11am.
Facilities 50-person cinema. Hire *Pinuccia*, Tresanton's 48-foot racing yacht with crew, or the hotel's inflatable rib (fast boat) or motor boat.
Smoking Considerate smoking allowed.
Kids Very welcome. A full-time nanny organises activities for kids during the summer months. Babysitters can be booked in advance.

In the know

Recommended rooms Room 1 is set apart and is often booked by honeymooners; Room 5 and 6 have a terrace; Room 29 in the Nook has a more modern interior and extra-luxurious bathroom.
Packing tips Beach shoes, binoculars, sou'wester if you're feeling boaty.
Also Sailing and windsurfing lessons can be arranged. Wellies, fishing rods and crabbing nets provided. Videos and board games will keep you amused on rainy days

Food & drink

In the hotel The restaurant specialises in fish and other local and organic produce.
Dress code People definitely make a bit of an effort in the evening.
Top table Weather permitting, book a table on the terrace; otherwise, a window table.
Last orders Kitchen closes at 9.30pm; after that, a cold supper can be arranged. The bar is open late.
Room service All night within reason (no lobster at 4am).
Breakfast 7.30am–10.30am.
Local restaurants **Driftwood** (01872 580644; see page 88) for wonderful fish and seafood. **Hunky Dory** in Falmouth (01326 212997) is a friendly spot for dinner.
Local pubs The **Victory Inn** (01326 270324) specialises in local seafood. The **Rising Sun** (01326 270233) for pub lunch and a pint. The bar at **Lugger Hotel** (01872 501322; see page 122).

Worth getting out of bed for

Indulge in a Thai massage, Indian head massage or Chavutti Thirumal massage – this is the only hotel in the UK where you can get this type of massage (applied by the feet to the entire body). Riding stables at Veryan (01872 501574). The Lost Gardens of Heligan, St Austell (01726 845100). Minack Open-air Theatre, Porthcurno (01736 810181): productions in summer months. Tate St Ives (01736 796226). The National Maritime Museum, Falmouth (01326 313388; www.nmmc.co.uk); the foot ferry leaves St Mawes harbour every 30 minutes.
Diary August: Falmouth Classics Regatta Week (www.falmouth-regatta.co.uk). British Surfing Championships in Newquay (www.surfnewquay.co.uk). October: Falmouth Oyster Festival for oyster tasting, washed down with champagne and Guinness.

Smith A free glass of champagne on arrival, and a large bar of exfoliating organic soap.

Get a room! Check availability and make reservations through www.mrandmrssmith.com.

Hotel Tresanton St Mawes, Truro, Cornwall (01326 270055)
info@tresanton.com; www.tresanton.com

be wary of anyon
love will last lon

'One should always
who promises their
er than a weekend'

Quentin Crisp

The Victoria at Holkham

SSMTWTF ■ MTWTSSMTWTFSSMT

you could be staying
with friends – if they
had a striking flair for
interior design

Style All the Raj
Setting Norfolk coast

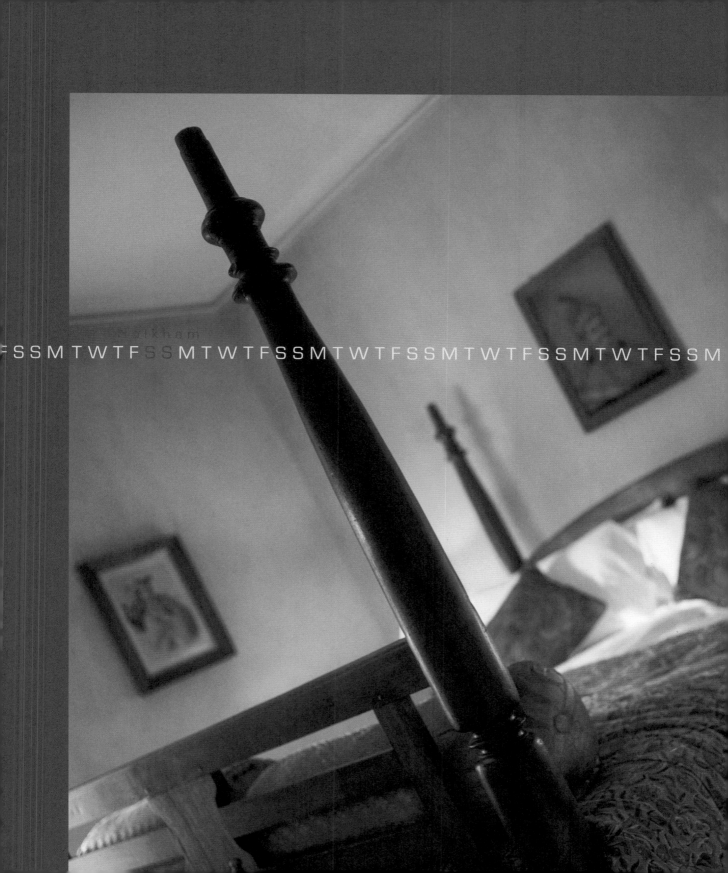

We arrived late for our dinner reservation at the Victoria, and only had time to throw our bags into our room before dashing down to the dining room. My chief concern on the way there had been whether a loose-lipped friend of Mr Smith's, well known to the hotel proprietors, might have told them we were no ordinary guests. It soon became clear he had stayed schtum. A bottle of champagne arrived so warm we wondered if it had been chilling in the bottom of the Aga with a couple of premature lambs. Opening it, the waitress wasted more fizz than Michael Schumacher at the end of a Grand Prix. However, amends were made so swiftly and unfussily, a cold one in an ice bucket appearing forthwith that, far from spoiling the evening, the episode seemed rather funny. A relaxed approach, it must be said, does suit the style of the hotel. With something of the feel of an old pub, it couldn't be a less demanding place for worn-out weekenders.

An old coaching inn on the fringes of the Holkham Hall estate, the 18th-century seat of the Earls of Leicester, the Victoria looks out onto marshland, and is directly opposite the most celebratedly stunning beach on Norfolk's coastline. It is a magical landscape to wake up to. The hotel was refurbished beautifully two years ago, and it is the decor, as well as the setting, that makes it so worth visiting. It certainly isn't 'look but don't touch', however: I never got the feeling that I couldn't put my feet up on the sofa, or kick off my shoes.

Our room was a confident mix of fashionably distressed and colourful Rajasthani furniture and interesting objects: old books, colonial bric-a-brac, intriguing bits and pieces. The bathroom was enjoyably spacious, with a pretty Victorian slipper bath, and specially commissioned handmade toiletries. The effect is very relaxing; you could be staying with friends – if they had a striking flair for interior design. In short, it is the antithesis of some cold, minimalist hotel rooms; and considerably better value for money.

We visited Holkham Hall the following morning, and explored its grounds: 3,000 acres of stunning parkland, with geese, deer, a lake, and an 18th-century icehouse. As we were driving away, a weasel ran in front of the car with fresh kill in its mouth, a once-in-a-lifetime sight, according to Mr Smith, who promptly leapt from the car in hot pursuit. A boat trip to the seal colony off Morston provided our second brush with nature.

That evening, we took a wonderful drive along the coast road to Itteringham for dinner at the Walpole Arms. The Walpole had been recommended by friends, and it more than lived up to our expectations. Mr George Batz, the manager, runs his restaurant with military precision, which was a stark contrast to the rather less strict management style of the Victoria. We ate and drank incredibly well, had a happy talk-filled evening, and all for under £70.

When we got back to the hotel at 11.30pm, Mr Smith was more than keen to head for the bar. We more or less had the place to ourselves; the house empties out in the evenings, and only residents remain. The Victoria pitches itself as a little bit of West London in the Norfolk countryside, but, delicious though the cocktails were, we have yet to find anywhere in Notting Hill that is so sleepy on a Saturday night. Again, it's more like spending a lazy weekend with friends. If you are happy to leave the hubbub behind, the Victoria's frayed, bohemian air and the glories of the East Anglian coastline make it one of the loveliest spots to stop and breathe the sweet sea air.

Need to know

Rooms 11. they also have three cottages which have kitchens and sitting rooms: Triumphal Arch (sleeps up to four), Palmer's Lodge (sleeps up to six), Cuckoo Lodge (sleeps up to four)
Rates £110–£200; lodges £110–£250.
Check-out 11am.
Kids Welcome. An extra child's bed or cot can be arranged in advance.
Also Smoking permitted in the lounge.

In the know

Recommended rooms The spacious neutral-toned Wash Room enjoys a greedy view over the marshes; the Raj Room is dark and cosy with a great four-poster; the lilac-coloured Marsh Room has a great view. All of the historic lodges are magnificent, but Cuckoo Lodge has a cute wooden kitchen with an Aga, as well as a big garden – ideal for of you're a *menage à quatre*.
Packing tips A kite for the beach; a hamper of cooking ingredients if you're staying in a lodge.
Also Shooting parties can be catered for.

Food & drink

In the hotel Fresh local food, including game and beef from the estate and seafood from the coast.
Dress code Relaxed.
Top table On the terrace in summer; a window table with view over the marsh in winter.
Last orders Food: 9.30pm (call ahead if you're going to be late). Bar: normal licensing hours, residents until late.
Room service Until last orders at the bar.
Breakfast 8am–10am.
Local restaurants The **Crown Hotel** in the Buttlands, Wells-next-the-Sea (01328 710209) is great for supper. The **Congham Hall** (01485 600250) serves Modern British and Sunday lunch in an elegant Georgian House.
Local pubs The **Hoste Arms** in Burnham Market (01328 738777) is a superb gastro experience. The **Walpole Arms** in Itteringham (01263 587258) is another gastropub for Sunday lunch. The **Hare Arms** at Stow Bardolph (01366 382229) is ideal for a pint.

Worth getting out of bed for

A stroll to Holkham Hall's stunning gardens, or the estate's golden beach, Holkham Gap. Seal trips, sailing and duck flighting can be organised by the hotel. Hire a boat on the Norfolk broads from George Smith & Sons (01603 782527; www.norfolkbroads.com). Karting at North Pickenham (01760 441777; www.anglia-karting.co.uk). Horse-riding at Bridlewood Livery & Riding Centre, Downham Market (01366 385923). Take the car of your dreams for a spin on the Snetterton Racetrack (0870 512 5250).
Diary October: Champion's Day at Newmarket (01638 663482; www.newmarketracecourses.co.uk).

Smith A complimentary half bottle of champagne on arrival.

Get a room! Check availability and make reservations through www.mrandmrssmith.com.

The Victoria at Holkham Park Road, Holkham, Norfolk (01328 711008)
victoria@holkham.co.uk; www.victoriaatholkham.co.uk

Westover Hall Hotel

M T W T F S S M T W T M T W T F S S M T W T F S S M T W T F S

Style Victorian magnificence
Setting South coast sea air

spectacular views
and bracing sea air
are heavenly to jaded
urban senses and lungs

A one-of-a kind Victorian mansion with a minstrel's gallery, stained-glass windows and big-sky views over the Solent and the Isle of Wight, Westover Hall is an amazing property in its own right. The warm atmosphere and just-so feel of its period interiors, though, is all thanks to its owners, Stewart Mechem and Nicola Musetti. Stewart and Nicola talk passionately of creating a superb 'home from home' for guests from the first minute they arrive (observing correctly that a bad first impression is difficult to recover from). And, indeed, the welcome we received when we drew up at Westover was so warm we were greeted by name before we'd even reached the front door. Our host led us into a staggering main hall, all oak panelling and Pre-Raphaelite stained glass, and from there to our room.

The Yellow Room is one of six (out of 12) to have a sea view. It has high ceilings, and a firm, if creaky, bed; the bathroom was similarly spacious, with nautical theming in the shape of a wooden model yacht (which we tried, unsuccessfully, to sail in the bath). Books and videos are supplied in case of inclement weather but, given the glorious sunshine streaming in, we headed straight for the beach. Usually, you can change in the hotel's own beach hut, but since it was was being refurbished, we padded through the splendid hall in shorts and T-shirts. We felt not in the least self-conscious; Westover Hall is a happy marriage of luxury and laissez-faire. It looks croquet, but it feels yoga.

On the beach, you can march as far as Hurst Castle if you want to, but we found it easy to linger, taking in the mesmerising sound of wave breaking on shingle, and the view across the yacht-studded Solent to the Isle of Wight. Should you wish to stride rather than stroll, you will need sturdy shoes to walk on the pebbles (mostly rounded, but with a few skimmers for the athletes

among us). I was ready to report that the sea was invitingly cool after my ankle-dip, until Mrs Smith scornfully pointed out a purposeful octogenarian wading into the water nearby. My competitive instincts awoken, I scorched *Baywatch*-style into the surf, beating the senior citizen to full immersion by a (grey) whisker, and quickly revised my temperature report to 'invigoratingly cold'. I soon acclimatised; however, I was still first out, and flushed with this back-to-back success, we repaired to the Yellow Room to change for dinner.

We kicked off with cocktails, olives and parsnip crisps in the formal but comfortable lounge at the front of the hotel, which is packed with stuffed armchairs and a huge fireplace. There's more than one spot to enjoy a drink at Westover: the small but beautifully balanced balcony room; the delightfully cool bar; and the outside terrace, all with fine sea views. The dining room is handsome, with more decorative windows and oak panelling, providing a contrast to Stewart's art and photographic collection. The atmosphere is intimate and relaxed.

Among what looked like three-foot wine glasses filled with fresh lilies, we ate impeccable sea-bass and succulent roast lamb (and a flaming pudding involving

Grand Marnier). Apparently, the menu changes daily, which almost seems a shame when they had it so perfect that evening, but I strongly suspect that the chef (the almost indecently youthful Matt Rock) repeats the feat each time. We staggered outside with the remnants of our wine, tastebuds buzzing, for a final moment with that superb view, before heading off to bed.

Fully refreshed in the morning, we found we had plenty of appetite to try out breakfast. As you would expect, the full medley is on offer, from cereals and yoghurts to cooked fare. Before leaving Westover, we had another saunter to the beach. It should be said that the hotel is not totally secluded and there is other housing nearby. Nevertheless, the spectacular view and bracing sea air are heavenly to jaded urban senses and lungs.

There are several 'things to do' in the area – walks on the coast or in the New Forest, visits to Lymington yacht marina, worthy boozers, such as the East End Arms. But, as we drove home past a mile-long queue of traffic heading south, we reflected that Westover is all about *not* having to do things. With just one night to play with, we were more than content to enjoy what Westover is so very good at: cuisine that would be hard to better anywhere; some of the finest views on the south coast, and, inside in Westover World, the unbeatable combination of beautiful surroundings and a relaxed, friendly atmosphere. Some home from home!

Reviewed by Mr & Mrs Smith

Need to know

Rooms 11 rooms and one suite.

Rates £150–£350, including breakfast and dinner; up to £470 for a family room (sleeps four).

Check-out 11am; midday by prior arrangement.

Facilities Beach hut for guest use; massage can be pre-booked.

Kids Babysitting and nanny, bookable in advance.

Also No smoking in bedrooms or restaurant.

In the know

Recommended rooms Three superior rooms with sea views. We liked the junior suite, room 7, room 6 for the view and room 5, a large seaview room.

Packing tips Beach accessories.

Also Dogs welcome.

Food & drink

In the hotel Superb Modern European food with a French influence.

Dress code Nautical but nice.

Top table Ask for a sea view.

Last orders Dinner: 8.45pm. Drinks: 12.30am.

Room service Until 10pm.

Breakfast 7.30am–9.30am; 10am at the weekends.

Local restaurants **Rouille** in Milford-on-Sea (01590 642340) is great for dinner. The **Mill** at Gordleton (01590 682219) for lunch in beautiful surroundings (ask for a garden view). **La Palette** on the seafront at Milford (01590 642646) is a relaxed and authentic French restaurant. If you fancy Italian, **Piccolo Mondo** (01590 643557) on the high street is perfect.

Local pubs Lymington: the **East End Arms** pub (01590 626223), owned by a member of Dire Straits, is a great place for lunch. The **Fisherman's Rest** (01590 678931) serves pub food at lunchtime (closed Sundays). **The Smugglers Inn** (01590 644414) is ideal for an afternoon pint.

Worth getting out of bed for

Horse-riding and biking can be arranged through the hotel. For autophiles, the Beaulieu National Motor Museum (01590 612345). A day trip to the Isle of Wight (www.iwight.com); the ferry gets to Lymington from Yarmouth (www.wightlink.co.uk) in half an hour. For absolutely anything boaty, speak to the Boat Club (01202 666616; www.boatclub.co.uk).

Diary July: watch the Admiral's Cup take place in the Solent (020 7493 2248; www.rorc.org) from the terrace of the George Hotel on the Isle of Wight. August: Cowes Week on the Isle of Wight (www.cowes.co.uk) for yacht racing, parties and fireworks. September: Southampton Boat Show (0115 912 9190; www.southamptonboatshow.com). 'Animal' Poole Windfest, Dorset (01202 707757; www.poolewindfest.co.uk).

Smith A complimentary bottle of wine with evening meal in the hotel restaurant.

Get a room! Check availability and make reservations through www.mrandmrssmith.com.

Westover Hall Hotel Park Lane, Milford-on-Sea, Lymington, Hampshire (01590 643044)
info@westoverhallhotel.com; www.westoverhallhotel.com

Whatley Manor

MTWTF ▬ MTWTSSMTWTFSSMTWTFSSMTW

Style Unadulterated luxury
Setting Landscaped Wiltshire gardens

feeling like robert wagner and
stephanie powers, we have our
own max to take care of us

Easton Grey

If naked mud-rubbing for two, in one of the country's swankiest new hotels, appeals to you, then welcome to Whatley Manor. At the end of a recently carved tree-lined driveway, we are met by a discreet set of gates that must have been purchased from NASA-gizmos.com, since they know who we are and open automatically. As we drive around the gravel courtyard, we listen rapt to its wonderfully expensive crunching sound, and the first 'oh, it's lovely' comes from the passenger seat.

We draw up, and a smartly dressed man appears in perfect synchronicity from the grade II-listed Cotswold stone façade. Another man flanks him to intercept our luggage. 'Good afternoon, sir, madam – welcome to Whatley Manor'. The score cards come up and it's a perfect ten, with both judges in full agreement.

It's a swift check-in, with a guided tour from our manager. That's right: you get your own manager, whom you can ring any time on his mobile. You also get your own mobile, so if you'd like a glass of something crisp and cold delivered to a well-chosen spot in the garden, consider it done. So, feeling like Robert Wagner and Stephanie Powers, with our own Max to take care of us, we're escorted to our room and left to our own devices. Our bags have arrived at the room before us (judges, again, quick to award top marks for style). The next wow is the view over the beautiful gardens, which lead to lush green meadows where cows graze. It is truly one of the best vistas I have ever seen from a hotel window.

Our room is a split-level suite, with stairs leading down to a marble-floored bathroom completely kitted out in white. The room itself is tastefully decorated and extremely elegant – neither too contemporary nor too classic. A super-king bed, Bang & Olufsen TVs in both

rooms, and a sound system that extends to a subwoofer built into the bath-tub is all extremely groovy.

We have a treatment booked at the spa in half an hour, so I've got time to try out the master remote that controls all the high-tech gadgetry. Lights on, lights off, radio on, TV off, play DVD... Brilliant: I would be quite happy staying in the room. Mrs Smith flicks through the hotel literature (not nearly as excited as I am by the techno wizardry, oddly enough). Stunning grounds to explore, 40-seater cinema, 24-hour room service, nothing too much trouble, original name of the house 'Twatley Manor'... This gem is too much for my schoolboy sense of humour, and it takes a swift drink from the minibar and a drag on my inhaler to calm me down.

Laughter barely subsided, we don our dressing gowns. Yellow has never been my colour, and the matching towelling slippers don't do much to help curb the chuckles, but we figure everyone must be wearing them spa-side. The Aquarias Spa is situated in the stable block of the building, and has one of the largest indoor/outdoor hydrotherapy pools in the UK, so the bumf reliably informs us. It's not designed for swimming, but it's perfect for lounging while you're pummelled by a variety of bubbling jets and miniature waterfalls. It's impressive, to say the least, and conducive to prolonged wallowing, especially given the views from the outside pool areas.

So, the naked mud bit. Mrs Smith has booked a treatment that involves both of us, starkers, rubbing two different kinds of rare, expensive mud all over each other. We then sit sweating in a sauna-style room and let the magic happen. Looking like a couple of outback kids that have spent a mucky three days trekking through the bush, we proceed to slip, slide and laugh for the next 20 minutes as the magic sludge rids us of those evil urban toxins. After the challenge of getting all the mud off, we did feel deeply cleansed and it is something I highly recommend – just don't tell the boys back home.

After changing into our eveningwear and descending for a perfect vodka tonic on the garden terrace, it's time to see what's cooking. The fine-dining restaurant isn't yet open; we're among the very first guests to experience Whatley, staying there in its first week as a hotel. We settle for Le Mazot, the more relaxed brassiere-style eatery. It's quite unlike the rest of the place: Whatley's Swiss owners have given it a 'top-of-the-mountain ski lodge' feel, which is unusual but just fine. The food is the star of the show; it is quite faultless. Head chef Martin Burge has had an illustrious career, perfecting his skills at Le Manoir and L'Ortolan.

We're left in no doubt that the fine dining would also be a triumph. We do sneak a look at the dining room and, once again, it is nothing like the rest of Whatley: no chalet vibe this time, but an outré look that is well-nigh impossible to describe. I'll try: red Japanese illustrations, printed onto fabric, covering the walls. And bright-green Venetian glass chandeliers. It's a little bit OTT, but you have been warned... If it's not exactly my taste, the rest of Whatley is lovely. The incredible grounds and cuisine – and the Mr & Mrs Mud experience – are more than enticing enough to lure us back (we've started saving already).

Reviewed by Mr & Mrs Smith

Need to know

Rooms 23.
Rates £275–£850, including breakfast.
Check-out Midday.
Facilities Aquarias Spa with hydrotherapy pool, thermal cabins, and small gym; 40-seat cinema.
All rooms Bang & Olufsen-fitted.
Kids Over-12s welcome.
Also Smoking permitted, except in the Dining Room.

In the know

Recommended rooms Rooms with garden views, especially 10 and 12. Room 2 has a chapel-like feel.
Packing tips Suitable attire for the spa.
Also Picnic hampers and rugs available on request.

Food & drink

In the hotel The Dining Room has recently been refurbished, and chef Martin Burge has been awarded a Michelin star for his French cuisine. Le Mazot is the Swiss-style brasserie. Snacks in the lounge areas, and a café in the spa.
Dress code Stealth wealth.
Top table The Dining Room: request a garden view. Le Mazot: a table away from the kitchen.
Last orders Food: 10pm.
Room service 24 hours.
Breakfast 7.30am–10.30am.
Local restaurants The **Old Bell** in Malmesbury (01666 822344) for lunch and dinner.
Calcot Manor near Tetbury (01666 890391) has two restaurants: the **Conservatory** for traditional food in a fine-dining setting and the **Gumstool** Inn for a rustic feel.
Local pubs The **Wild Duck** in Ewen (01285 770310) is an excellent local pub.
The **Village Pub** in Barnsley (01285 740 421) has gastro food and an inventive wine list.

Worth getting out of bed for

Have a spin in a racing car or off-roader at Castle Coombe race circuit (0870 2408385; www.castlecombecircuit.co.uk). For a flying lesson or trip in a microlight, contact Kemble Flying Club (01285 770077; www.kembleflyingclub.com). Westonbirt Arboretum has a fine tree and wild-flower collection (01666 881208; www.westonbirtarboretum.com). Beaufort Polo Club, favoured by the Prince of Wales and his sons (01666 880510; wwwbeaufortpoloclub.co.uk).
Diary March: Cheltenham Festival and the Gold Cup (01242 537642; www.cheltenham.co.uk). April/May: Badminton Horse Trials (01454 218272; www.badminton-horse.co.uk). August: the British Horse Trial Championships, Gatcombe Park (01937 5411811; www.gatcombe-horse.co.uk).

Smith A complimentary signature Whatley Manor cocktail for each day of your stay.

Get a room! Check availability and make reservations through www.mrandmrssmith.com.

Whatley Manor Easton Grey, Malmesbury, Wiltshire (01666 822888)
reservations@whatleymanor.com; www.whatleymanor.com

Scotland

Ireland

Wales

England

A lot of the world's sights can be overhyped and disappointing, but natural wonders don't get much more magical than those hexagonal dark-stone steps at low tide

Kilgraney House

Style
Setting

beautiful scenes of trees and rolling fields
prepare you for the hotel's elegance

Bagenalstown

TWTFSSMTWTFSSMTWTFSSMTWTFSSMTWTFSSMT

We picked up a Renault Scenic at Dublin airport, which gave us the feeling we should be on a school run. I'd been thinking of something a little flasher, obviously, but there was plenty of leg room, at least. It was a beautiful day, and, as we headed south towards Kilkenny, the sun poured in through the double sunroof (bonus point for the Scenic). Turning on the radio, we caught a local Name That Sound competition. The DJ was just reminding a contestant that the sound in question had been a mystery for a record four days. A clinking noise was relayed, and the caller said, in the broadest of accents: 'Well, it's the lid being replaced either on a teapot or on a cookie jar.' A noticeable perk in the DJ's voice revealed that one of these was, in fact, the right answer. 'So, Paddy... (we are not making this up) ...what's it to be: the teapot or the cookie jar?' The excitement mounted as Paddy changed his mind several times.

We in the car were shouting 'Teapot! Teapot!' as we drove down the motorway at 70mph (top speed for the Scenic: deduct bonus point). After several suspenseful minutes, Paddy plumped for the teapot. After a full trumpet fanfare, the DJ announced the prize – dinner for two at what sounded like the local fish 'n' chip shop. Quite brilliant.

The nearer we got to Kilkenny, the prettier the countryside became; after one and a half hours on the road, we arrived in County Carlow. The drive to Kilgraney House, through beautiful scenes of trees and rolling fields, prepares you for the elegant hotel itself. Its interior has been decorated with surprising touches by Bryan and Martin, the owners and our hosts for the night, who made us feel most welcome and happy to be there. The reception looks like the front hall of a very attractive home, which is, essentially, what it is; we later found out that the paintings and objects that give the Georgian house a well-travelled and individual feel are mainly from the Philippines, where Bryan and Martin used to work. Our room was bright and spacious, done out in natural linens, creams and olive green.

We were told we had the choice of dining à deux, or communally. The first option would place us in a smaller room off the main dining room; the communal experience meant eating with the other hotel residents. Yikes! For city-dwellers like us, who don't say hello to their neighbours, the prospect of socialising with complete strangers was daunting. However, when in Ireland... We plucked up courage, and decided to be convivial. We were offered afternoon tea on the lawn, and basked in the last of the sun's rays before getting ready for our sociable dinner.

After rehearsing repartee in the bath and to the mirror, we descended to meet our fellow guests for an aperitif downstairs, before filing into the dining room for our six-course set menu. After a couple of drinks, the conversation flowed. We found ourselves with two artists, a film student, and a couple who refused to tell us what they did (we reckoned KGB, professional S&M party organisers, or hotel reviewers). It turned out to be a most enjoyable evening. We covered: the euro, potato blight, Albania, painting holidays in Spain and Venezuela, and how to get rid of slugs in an eco-friendly way. The food, which included delicious wild venison, was faultless. Bryan and Martin shared the hosting and cooking, and laughed at our attempts to bribe our fellow guests to reveal what they did. They'd obviously been through the same line of questioning the previous night and couldn't bear to go through it again. Which brings us on to our tip of the trip – we suggest going solo the first night, and communal the second; that way, you have plenty to talk about.

Coffee and liqueurs were served in the sitting room. An open fire and accommodating sofas made it so relaxing – elegant but informal – that at one point I nearly got up to put the kettle on myself. After a wonderful night's sleep (the bed was super-comfortable, if a little smaller than we're used to), we woke in time for breakfast, where we proceeded to consume, between us, fresh pancakes with home-made orange crème fraîche, a full Irish, and scrambled eggs with smoked salmon – a true tribute to Bryan and Martin's kitchen, since we had been planning on no more than a coffee and the smell of croissant.

On the way home, we had been told we must have a drop of the black stuff at O'Sheas, which must be one of the most fantastically old-fashioned pubs we've ever been to. Not only does it sell a fine glass of Guinness, but it also doubles as an electrical shop, so ordering a pint and a pack of lightbulbs isn't uncommon. We were sorry to leave the gentle weirdness of County Carlow, and the warmth of Kilgraney House. It already has something of a cult following, but Bryan and Martin have great plans for the place, including a mini spa and further rooms. We are confident that whatever they do will be perfect in every detail – and even more confident that it won't be long until we return.

Reviewed by Mr & Mrs Smith

Need to know

Rooms Six in the house, two apartments.
Rates €130–€240.
Check-out Midday.
Facilities Aroma Spa and treatment rooms (pre-arrange appointments).
Kids Under-12s not encouraged.
Also Smoking permitted in the lounge.

In the know

Recommended rooms The African and Buddha rooms, for their big beds. Herb and Loft courtyard suites overlook the medicinal herb garden. The Philippine room has a garden view and Church has the best bathroom.
Packing tips Passport and euros, depending on where you're travelling from.
Also Kilgraney takes guests Thursday, Friday, Saturday and Sunday nights between March and November.

Food & drink

In the hotel Your hosts serve a six-course table d'hôte dinner.
Dress code Informal elegance.
Top table If you dine privately, a table by the window.
Last orders Dinner is served at 8.00pm. Last drinks served 12.30am.
Room service Not available.
Breakfast 8.30am–10.30am.
Local restaurants Kilkenny: **Zuni** (+353 (0) 56 772 3999) does Modern European food. **Kendal's** (+353 (0) 56 777 3073) at Mount Juliet Golf Course is a smart restaurant serving Irish and European dishes. The **Kilkenny Design Centre** (+353 (0) 56 772 2118) has a brasserie. For French food, try **Pordylos** (+353 (0) 56 777 0660).
Local bars/pubs **O'Sheas** in Borris (+353 (0) 59 977 3106) is a pub/hardware store that's great for a pint. The **Lord Bagenal** (+353 (0) 59 972 1668) is good for Sunday lunch. In Kilkenny, the **Marble City Bar** (+353 (0) 56 776 1143) is a contemporary bar serving food. **Tynan's Bar** at Bridge House (+353 (0) 56 772 1291) is another traditional pub.

Worth getting out of bed for

A licence for coarse fishing on the River Barrow can be arranged by the tackle shop in Bagenalstown. Quad-biking with Country Quads (+353 (0) 50 324624). Horse-riding at Carrigbeg Riding Stables (+ 353 (0) 50 321962). Diary March: St Patrick's Day (www.st-patricks-day.com). May: The Cat Laughs Comedy Festival (www.thecatlaughs.com) August: Kilkenny Arts Festival (www.kilkennyarts.ie). June: Eigse Arts Festival (www.eigsecarlow.com). October: Wexford Opera Festival (+353 (0) 53 22144; www.wexfordopera.com).

Smith Complimentary use of the Aroma Spa with a two-night, two-dinners stay; pre-booking essential.

Get a room! Check availability and make reservations through www.mrandmrssmith.com.

Kilgraney House Bagenalstown, County Carlow, Ireland +353 (0) 59 977 5283
info@kilgraneyhouse.com; www.kilgraneyhouse.com

The Morrison

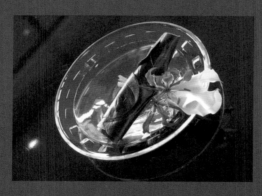

MTWTFSSMTWTFSSM

Style John Rocha genius
Setting Riverside Dublin

a perfect weekend
destination if you want
a healthy dose of
culture, a large helping
of pudding and a nice
big afternoon nap

Dublin

On the north side of the Liffey, with views across to the opposite bank of the river, the Morrison is one of Dublin's most stylish hotels. Home-grown fashion designer John Rocha was responsible for its interior so it is, unsurprisingly, very striking. It was immediately apparent that Rocha has struck the right balance between creative and comfortable. Dark-wood floors, cream walls, chocolate-brown suede cubes and red tie-dye velvet throws and cushions make the hotel as pleasing to the eye as it is on the derrière – unusual for a designer hotel, where it's usually one or the other.

What did we expect from a long weekend in Dublin? Guinness, of course. Cobbled streets, without question. Bookshops flogging the complete works of James Joyce, undoubtedly. Rain, most probably. And if we were really unlucky, bumping into members of Westlife. But we discovered there's a lot more to this cosy, cultivated and captivating city than bad weather, booze, books and boy bands. Best of all, Dublin lets you daintily dip into its offerings as and when you feel like it, and the Morrison is the perfect base.

The atmosphere of the hotel is very relaxing, almost sleepy. Lively, up-at-the-crack-of-dawn types might find the hotel, and the whole of Dublin, a little disconcerting, but we intended to embrace its philosophy and spend as much of the weekend in bed as we could. So it was important to find out as soon as we arrived if they had that part right. The beds, I'm happy to report, were indeed heavenly: big and bouncy with Frette linen sheets, goosedown pillows and lots of bedside buttons so you don't even have to move much. The bathroom is also a delight. Enormous, packed with Molton Brown goodies, it even has a shower with room enough for two. (Three, indeed, if you're feeling particularly convivial).

The second most important item on our checklist is the dining. The room-service menu, also served in the bar, is ample, but it was in the restaurant, Halo, that the Morrison excelled itself. Halo features an Asian fusion menu, and is in a wonderful space with a double-height ceiling. Presentation was a little heavy on the squiggles of sauce and gold-leaf flourishes for simple tastes, but it was of high quality and served by charming staff. Hardly for the budget-conscious, it was well worth at least one visit during our stay. The wine list was compact but well chosen, featuring my current favourite, the Lebanese Chateau Musar 1996.

When I asked for the bill from a member of the extraordinarily helpful staff, she suggested a nightcap in the bar. Saturdays see the two bar areas get really lively, with a young, fashionable crowd packing into every pocket and corner. And, always a bonus, the lighting is very, very low. Even after too many Cosmopolitans and too little sleep, the pop-band groupies littering the bar area won't look too frightening on a Sunday morning.

Fortunately for anyone nursing a hangover, Dublin is big on breakfasts. Served in the hotel until a civilised 11am, ours helped us build up the energy to move beyond our bedroom, and we discovered many attractions within walking distance. Just over the bridge, the Temple Bar area is packed with design and furniture stores, bars and cafés. Venturing further, we took a stroll through the grounds of Trinity College before heading off for some shopping at Brown Thomas, the designer-packed department store. Had we been feeling especially energetic, we could have paid a visit to the Guinness Store House. There, when you've done the rounds, you get a free pint served in a glass-walled room at the top of a tower overlooking the whole of Dublin. We decided our favourite view was still the one from our bedroom – a pint of the black stuff but a room-service call away. If you want a healthy dose of culture, a large helping of pudding and a nice big afternoon nap, Dublin is the perfect weekend destination – and what better rendezvous than the Morrison?

Reviewed by Jeremy Langmead

Need to know

Rooms 138 including a penthouse and six suites.
Rates €270; suites from €445; penthouse €1,460.
Check-out Midday
Facilities Temporary membership of a local gym (pre-arrange treatments).
Kids Children are welcome: babysitters and high chairs available.

In the know

Recommended rooms Eight rooms have views over the Liffey (€40 supplement).
Packing tips Drinking boots.
Also The concierges at the Morrison are a mine of information and can be helpful with guestlists,
so make friends early. Don't forget your euros.

Food & drink

In the hotel Their contemporary restaurant serves a fusion of world cuisine; tapas menu available
from 12pm until 11pm.
Dress code City glamour.
Top table One on the edge of the mezzanine.
Last orders Food: 10.15pm (later if busy). The café bar: 11.30pm. Ground-floor bar: midnight.
Room service 24 hour.
Breakfast 7am–10.30am.
Local restaurants **Browne's** brasserie (+353 (0)1 638 3939) for French cooking in a romantic
setting. **Jacob's Ladder** (+353 (0)1 670 3865) and **Chapter One** (+353 (0)1 873 2266) for
modern Irish cuisine. **Eden** (+353 (0)1 670 5372) for seasonal, organic food.
Local bars **Spy** (+353 (0)1 677 0014) is a cool NY-style bar and club. The **Café en Seine**
(+353 (0)1 677 4567) has the longest bar imaginable.
Dawson Lounge (+353 (0) 677 5909) is supposedly the smallest pub in Ireland.
Local pubs **Kehoe's** (+353 (0)1 677 8312) in South Anne Street is a traditional pub.
Duke's of Duke St (+353 (0)1 679 9553) is one of Dublin's many literary drinking dens.
The best brunches are at the **Mermaid Café** (+353 (0)1 670 8236) on Dame Street, or
the **Elephant & Castle** (+353 (0)1 679 3121) in Temple Bar.

Worth getting out of bed for

Dublin is home to thousands of musicians and bands, so check local listings (www.dublin.local.ie).
The Guinness factory tour (+353 (0)1 408 4800; www.guinness-storehouse.com).
Diary March: St Patrick's Day (www.stpatricksday.ie). July: the Witnness music festival
(www.witnness.com).

 A complimentary bottle of house wine when dining, plus full Irish breakfast.

Get a room! Check availability and make reservations through www.mrandmrssmith.com.

The Morrison Lower Ormond Quay, Dublin, Ireland (+353 (0)1 887 2400)
info@morrisonhotel.ie; www.morrisonhotel.ie

TENsq

SSMTWTF MTWTFSSMTWTFSSMT

Style Contemporary with an Asian accent.
Setting Buzzing Belfast

Belfast

SSMTWTFSSMTWTFSSMTWTFSSM

definitely living up to its reputation as belfast's coolest hotel

When we arrived in Belfast, it was a grey old day, but a chatty cab driver boosted our morale with anecdotes and nuggets of local history. As part of his en route commentary he proudly informed us that the *Titanic* had been built here – the first surprise of the trip. It was only 15 minutes from the airport to the hotel and when we got there the receptionist seemed so genuinely pleased to see us, our spirits were, once again, lifted.

We made our way to our room, a large contemporary space with an Asian influence (red-painted ostrich eggs and single orchids in glass vases) and a huge low-slung bed with a dark wood frame and red cushioned headboard – very stylish. Having examined all the mod cons (Bang & Olufsen TV, dimmable lights, heating controls) and purred over the well-stocked minibar and bathroom goodies (there are additional Molton Brown Pamper Gift Boxes available to buy) and marvelled at the Perspex-enclosed hay-bale coffee table, we decided that TENsq, designed by the people who brought us London's celeb favourite, the Met Bar, was definitely living up to its reputation as Belfast's coolest hotel.

The hotel has a ground-floor bar, which transforms into a lively DJ-fuelled hangout, but we were in the mood for something a little more relaxed. Upstairs, the second-floor events suite, Porcelain, offers a refined and sophisticated lounge where a resident pianist has been known to play during dinner (and, yes, we did request a tune or two without feeling naff – he played Coldplay's 'Clocks' for us and Elton John's 'Tiny Dancer'. I know, there's still no excuse). It made a very enjoyable change to the usual *Café Del Mar* or *Now That's What I Call Chill-out* offerings. We were even informed that the likes of Andrea Corr and Moby have been known to perform impromptu live sets. So, while we were waiting for Westlife to appear, we settled down to wait for our bistro-style nosh.

A few nightcaps later, we staggered to our large, comfortable bed and its oversized goose-down pillows. In the morning, after a very full Irish breakfast, we decided to take in a bit of local history. From what we could make out, the taxi drivers have all diversified and double up as tour guides, taking visitors round the murals in the divided parts of the city. Utterly fascinated, we hung on our cabbie's every word for the entire hour. We drove past curfew gates that shut every night at 10pm; 50-foot walls and barriers that still separate Republican and Loyalist families; small memorials along the roadside, and bullet-proof windows still in place – all sad reminders of the rifts that remain, even if they're less volatile than in the past. By now on good terms with our driver, we decided to go the full touristy hog and

head out to Giant's Causeway, about an hour and a half
outside the city. A lot of the world's sights can be
overhyped and disappointing, but natural wonders
don't get much more magical than those hexagonal
dark-stone steps at low tide.

Sadly, our first visit to Belfast was to be a fleeting
one; sad because there was so much more to see.
Belfast may not seem an obvious choice for a
romantic weekend away, but it definitely delivered,
giving us a quite unexpected experience. With major
changes going on around the city, and TENsq the
perfect base for discovering its diversity, it is has truly
become a destination not to be missed. So get yourself
there (or be, erm, square).

Reviewed by Mr & Mrs Smith

Need to know

Rooms 23 rooms, including one mini-suite.
Rates £160–£240 including breakfast.
Check-out Midday.
Facilities Beauty treatments can be arranged. Discounts at Andrew Mulvenna health club.
Kids Welcome; high chairs available.

In the know

Recommended rooms One of the two corner rooms, which are bigger than the rest.
Packing tips Sturdy shoes for the Giant's Causeway.
Also Belfast open on a Sunday; this also goes for within TENsq.

Food & drink

In the hotel The Porcelain Restaurant, Bar Red and China Club have changed: the hotel has a new Grill Room & Bar which is the latest addition to Belfast's burgeoning social scene, and it fuses tradition and city-centre style. The menu offers simple traditional dishes, and bistro favourites, prepared with a modern twist. There is live music in the bar on Wednesday and Sunday nights; private dining is possible in the first-floor Porcelain events suites.
Dress code City chic.
Top table Banquette under the window.
Last orders The Grill Room: 10pm weekdays; 10.30pm weekends, but the bar is open all week.
Room service 24 hours.
Breakfast 7am–10am; 8am–11.30am on Saturdays; 8am–1pm on Sunday.
Local restaurants Celebrity chefs the Rankins run Irish/Asian **Cayenne** (02890 331532) which is open on Sundays. The Michelin-starred **Deane's Restaurant** (02890 560000) does fusion cuisine.
Local bars **TaTu** (02890 380818) is one of Belfast's coolest places to go for a cocktail.
Local pubs The **Crown Bar** (02890 279901) has a perfectly preserved Victorian pub interior. **Robinsons** (02890 247447) is a Belfast institution, with traditional music.

Worth getting out of bed for

Casement Park (02890 605868) is the home of Gaelic football, and also where hurling matches take place. Political taxi tours of the murals can be arranged through the hotel. The Giant's Causeway (an hour and a half away) is worth the drive (www.giantscausewayofficialguide.com).
Diary May: Belfast Film Festival (02890 325913; www.belfastfilmfestival.org). The Balmoral Show (02890 665225; www.balmoralshow.co.uk) – Northern Island's premier Agricultural Show. October/ November: Belfast Festival, covering all art forms (02890 272626; www.belfastfestival.com).

 A complimentary bottle of wine with supper in the restaurant (please make sure you mention your Smithcard when booking your table).

Get a room! Check availability and make reservations through www.mrandmrssmith.com.

TENsq 10 Donegall Square South, Belfast, County Antrim, Northern Ireland (02890 241001) reservations@tensquare.co.uk; www.tensquare.co.uk

Scotland

Ireland

Wales

England

One Devonshire Gardens

S S M T W T F ■ M T W T F S S M T W T F S S M T

Style Five-star intimate grandeur
Setting Glasgow's West End

wherever you
are in one
devonshire,
personal
service
follows you

Glasgow

F S S M T W T F S S M T W T F S S M T W T F S S M T W T F S S M

Located off the main artery of Glasgow's West End, One Devonshire Gardens is a converted terrace of blond sandstone houses. The entrance resembles that of a smart members' establishment, and as with a private club, you can't just walk on in. The front door is always locked, and a brass plaque reads: 'Please ring for personal attention.' When we did, a cheery member of staff ran – oh yes, ran – to let us in.

There's a wise saying about the art of conversation: people don't just want to be charmed; they want to be charming. The same goes for hotels. People don't just want to stay in a classy place; they want to *be* classy. Some upmarket places can leave you feeling rather insecure, as though you're not posh enough to be there. Fortunately, that's not the case at the hotel where pop stars, actors and big boys of business rest their heads when they're in Glasgow. We might not have the fame, fortune or dancing ability of previous guests such as Michael Jackson and Kylie, but we were made to feel just as special, right from the get-go.

Although the interior has been exquisitely designed, it has a very homely feel to it (perhaps because the building did once provide several dwellings). Unlike many hotels with a comparable number of bedrooms (it has 38), One Devonshire retains an intimate atmosphere. And wherever you are in One Devonshire, personal service follows you. A friendly note from the manager awaited us in the bedroom, next to an extraordinary rectangular bowl of apples.

Our room was comfortably large and, like the rest of the hotel, it was sophisticated in a pleasingly understated way. The four-poster bed looked spectacular and we couldn't wait to get in it. But anyone planning a saucy weekend, beware: once you get horizontal, sleep is likely to become the most tempting option. We resisted the pull of the crisp white sheets, and set off to take advantage of the fine dining on offer. After all, it's not every day you get to have lunch from one of Gordon Ramsay's kitchens.

As you'd expect from a restaurant where the set lunch menu costs £35 a head, the food at Amaryllis was delightful. My braised beef was so tender I could have broken it up with my bare hands.

Two impeccably stylish drawing rooms are the location for pre-dinner drinks and quiet daytime coffees – sometimes a little too quiet. We weren't desperate to talk raucously about unsavoury medical complaints, but our snug proximity to the other guests did conjure up fantasies about whoopee cushions and naked handstands, so we thought we'd get out and explore the neighbourhood. We went strolling among the giant Venus fly-traps of the Botanic Gardens, not far from the hotel, and then bumbled around cobbled Ashton Lane enjoying its relaxed bars and restaurants and a rather eccentric shopping arcade.

For dinner, we chose the Devonshire's other eatery, House 5. The restaurant shares the informal luxury ethos of Amaryllis, although House 5's warm colours and open fire make it a cosier proposition. The atmosphere was jovial, thanks to friendly, efficient waiting staff. Here, the sharp-suited seem to sit perfectly comfortably beside arty types. The food was very good, and made a slightly less formal alternative to Amaryllis; we couldn't wait to get back to House 5 the next morning for its fantastic Scottish cooked breakfast. When we did, we weren't disappointed; the portions aren't over-the-top, so you can enjoy a quality fry-up without feeling too abused afterwards.

Bearing in mind the calibre of celeb guests that One Devonshire attracts, the staff is clearly used to some serious rock 'n' roll tour antics. When we asked the night receptionist if it would be all right for a couple of pals to swing by our room later that night, he didn't bat an eyelid. 'As long as you don't disturb anyone, it's up to you what you want to do in your room, sir,' he said, with a twinkle in his eye. If he didn't believe our innocent story about wanting to watch a film, he didn't say so. But to be honest, any mischievous plans we might have had before we arrived had been shattered by the time we got to One Devonshire. We just wanted to curl up on our room's big comfortable sofa and watch DVDs on the large flat-screen telly. Hardly rock-star behaviour, but with so much comfort and luxury surrounding us, forget partying all night and chucking the telly out the window – staying in is the new going out.

Need to know

Rooms 35, and the two-bedroomed Mews Suite, which sleeps up to six.
Rates £150–£925.
Check-out Midday, but flexible.
Facilities Residents-only gym, in-room spa treatments, personal trainer by arrangement.
Kids Welcome, although no special facilities.

In the know

Recommended rooms Room 29: luxury penthouse suite with Jacuzzi bath, power shower, cinema-screen TV.
Room 21: four-poster bed, wooden fireplace and antiques. Rooms 2, 9, 11: grand suites. Room 23 and
House 5 rooms are more traditional, so ask for a more contemporary room if you want one. The Mews
Suite has two king-size bedrooms, two lounges and a dining room, as well as two bathrooms, a Jacuzzi,
sauna and gym and bar facilities.
Packing tips DVDs, CDs.
Also Restaurant reservations are advisable at the weekend, as is hiring a car if you want to escape the city.

Food & drink

In the hotel Award-winning No. 5 Restaurant serves contemporary European fine dining. Room Glasgow is a
modern lounge bar restaurant offering British classics prepared with modern-minded finesse.
Dress code Err on the side of formal.
Top table Room Glasgow: by the window. No. 5: table by the window.
Last orders Food: 9.15pm. Food in the bar: 9.30pm. Bar open all night for residents.
Room service 24 hours.
Breakfast 7am–10am. Continental breakfast in bed if requested.
Local restaurants Glasgow institution **Rogano** (0141 248 4055) is an art deco seafood restaurant. **Gamba**
(0141 572 0899), another fish restaurant, has a simple, exquisite menu. **Amber Regent** (0141 331 1655)
specialises in Cantonese and Szechuan cuisine. **Opus** (0141 204 1150) is a modern fine-dining experience
and has a late bar with great cocktails. **Zinc** (0141 225 56200) for a meal in stylish surrounds.
Local bars **Tiger Tiger** (0141 553 4888) late-night bar and nightclub is open until 3am at weekends.
Local pubs **Uisge Beatha** (pronounced oosh-ke-bar) (0141 564 1596), means 'water of life' in Gaelic
and, like the whisky it refers to, has a distinctly Scottish flavour. **Loch Fyne Oyster Bar** (01499 600217),
is a 45-minute drive from the city, but well worth the trip for the food and location.

Worth getting out of bed for

Glasgow is home to Scottish Opera, Royal Scottish National Orchestra, the Burrell Collection (art objects
from around the world) and the Lighthouse (where a Charles Rennie Mackintosh conversion houses a variety
of dynamic exhibitions); see www.visitscotland.com for details. Shopping: designer labels at the Italian
Centre; exclusive and upmarket brands in Princes Square; bohemian boutiques on Byres Road. For beauty
and tranquillity, head for Loch Lomond, the largest freshwater lake in the UK, only 30 minutes by car.
Diary April: Glasgow Art Fair: view, buy and sell contemporary art (0141 221 0049; www.glasgowartfair.com).
June: Glasgow's annual Jazz Festival (www.jazzfest.co.uk); Glasgow Art Fair; Bard in the Botanics Festival.

Smith Room upgrade subject to availability. A free morning paper and late check-out (normally £50).

Get a room! Check availability and make reservations through www.mrandmrssmith.com.

One Devonshire Gardens 1 Devonshire Gardens, Glasgow (0141 339 2001)
reservations@onedevonshiregardens.com; www.onedevonshiregardens.com

Drive through breathtaking scenery – lochs, mountains, wild deer

this is better than the
treatment I get at my
folks' house at christmas

Pool House

MTWTFSSMTWTF■MTWTFSSMTWTFSSMTWTFSSM

Style Traditional Scottish home
Setting Shores of Loch Ewe

TFSSMTWTFSSMTWTFSSMTWTFSSMTWTFSS

If the far-flung corners of Scotland seem a long way away, think again. We jumped on a plane to Inverness, collected a car from SRW (Sharp's Reliable Wrecks) and, after an hour and a half's drive through breathtaking scenery – lochs, mountains, wild deer – we were at Pool House.

Arriving tired, we didn't get to see much of the hotel that night, but we were given a very warm welcome indeed, and felt instantly like part of the family. Shown to our room, we discovered an open log fire, a huge 19th-century four-poster bed and antique throws. 'Rooms' barely does Pool House justice – city-dwellers live in less space; these are more like apartments. A few years ago the decision was made to transform 17 bedrooms into six luxury suites. Each was given a nautical theme, and the Diadem, where we stayed, is in the style of a first-class cabin on the *Titanic*. If an original tile mounted on the wall sounds something, brace yourself for the spacious bathrooms: ours contained a Victorian bath dating from 1875, one of only three of its kind in the world.

Pool House is full of passion – not in the sense that it's a typical honeymoon retreat, but because the wine, the food and the decor have become a vocation for a family who have searched the corners of the earth for the furniture. And the hotel's personality extends from the inanimate to the human fixtures. Pool House is run by sisters Elizabeth and Mhairi (her husband is the fantastic chef); father Peter is there to advise you on which of his whiskys will suit your mood. Meanwhile, mother Margaret keeps an eye out to make sure you are as comfortable as can be.

A world away from slick young barmen in contemporary hotels mixing up fancy cocktails, the Harrisons make you feel as though you've been invited into their home. We enjoyed a pre-dinner drink and some delicious canapés in the best seat in the house: the sofa in the living room. (The atmosphere is so relaxing that the owners regularly hear soft snoring emanating from it.) Too captivated by the sunset view to nod off, we admired the inspiration for the hotel's name. Just feet from the house, the river meets the ocean, and a pool forms. Here, salmon gather before swimming out to sea.

We were delighted we'd set aside a few hours for dinner; taking in our surroundings was as much of an experience to be savoured as the six-course meal. Murals, oversized candelabras and even a seven-foot circular compass in gold leaf (hand-painted by the Harrison sisters) provide a sublime backdrop for a gastronomic extravaganza made entirely from local produce. John Moir, the chef, has his own vegetable garden, chickens, pigs and geese, and venison, scallops and salmon are all caught locally. As for drinking, Peter has a cellar of more than 400 malt whiskys, 60 of which are sold by the glass. We couldn't resist a whole bottle, knowing we could take home what was left as a souvenir, the wine list ranges from £20 to £330 a pop.

In spite of our indulgence at supper, when it came to breakfast the next morning, the spread was still irresistible. It was a good job we had plans to get some exercise. And we knew how many layers to put on before stepping outside, thanks to a message accompanying our hot-water bottles at bedtime. 'I am Oscar the Otter – if you do not wish to be disturbed, please place me outside your door. Should you wish to go otter-spotting, the weather forecast suggests snowy showers tomorrow. Wrap up warm!' This is better than the treatment I get at my folks' house at Christmas. Maybe they'll adopt us.

We woke up to the most beautiful view of the sea. The marine option was to go whale-watching and look for porpoises, but because of choppy waves we chose to stretch our legs on land. Besides, we'd already volunteered to take the hotel's nine-year-old collie, Scampi, for a stroll. Had we been feeling lazy, a snooker table, a stack of books and games and a few drams of whisky would have kept us just as happy back at the hotel. Luckily for our waistlines, it was as much fun burning calories as it had been consuming them. The only hard part was saying goodbye to the wild beauty of the coast, Pool House and the Harrison family; Scotland's north-west would be a chillier place without them.

Reviewed by Mr and Mrs Smith

Need to know

Rooms Eight double suites, all with sea views.
Rates £295–£550, including full Scottish breakfast and complimentary tea and sherry.
Check-out Midday, but any convenient time close to this is fine.
Facilities Full-size billiards table and malt whisky room; massage by arrangement.
Kids Over-16s welcomed, but really this is a place for couples.

In the know

Room recommendations All the suites have fantastic water views. Our favourite is the Diadem: very intimate, with its own fireplace. The Boat House, Whimbrel, is your own 'gingerbread cottage', and as romantic as can be, thanks to a four-poster and a bath big enough for two. If you fancy stepping into the style of a Russian dacha, Bluebell is fit for a tsar.
Packing tips Walking boots and binoculars are essential.
Also A car for exploring is crucial: you can rent a car from SRW (Sharp's Reliable Wrecks) at Inverness airport (01463 236694). They'll meet you with the keys at arrivals if you pre-book.

Food & drink

In the hotel Dinner is a must, and you'll be unlikely to want a big lunch the next day.
Dress code Unshowy and warm.
Local restaurants Lunch at the **Kishorn Seafood Bar** (01520 733240) for fresh mussels with garlic butter (summer only). **Bridge Cottage Café and Gallery** on the main street (01445 781335) for delicious homemade soups and amazing cakes.
Local pub The **Badachro Inn** in Badachro (01445 741255) on the edge of the water; the **Old Inn** (01445 712006) in Gaerloch on the fishing harbour serves real ales. **Grumble Inn** (01445 771212): where else this side of the equator can you have a pint with emus and wallabies?
Also Have tea across the water in the National Trust tropical gardens.

Worth getting out of bed for

Spend a day getting to grips with hawks (01445 760204). Take a walk to the site of the World War II plane crash. Give the hotel two days' notice and they can arrange whisky tasting at Glen Ord Distillery. In the summer, learn yacht sailing, or go power-boating with a qualified instructor. Take a fast boat to the Summer Isles for a picnic. Visit the Isle Maree: sail across to this second seat of Christianity to see Viking graves. See a porpoise from the 30-foot yacht Ventura (01445 781729).
Diary July: Gairloch sheepdog trials (01445 712412) – watch the dogs in action. August: Assynt Highland Games Culag Park at Lochinver (01571 844647; www.albagames.co.uk) for highland dancing, piping, and salmon and trout fly-casting championships; Duck Race, when hundreds of rubber ducks are floated down the river in biannual watery madness.

Smith A complimentary boudoir box containing all sorts of treats for him and her.

Get a room! Check availability and make reservations through www.mrandmrssmith.com.

Pool House By Inverewe Garden, Poolewe, Wester Ross (01445 781272)
enquiries@poolhousehotel.com; www.poolhousehotel.com

Rick's

M T W T F ⬤ M T W T F S S M T W T F S S M T W T

Style Contemporary cocktail bar
Setting The heart of Edinburgh

Edinburgh
SMTWTFSSMTWTFS

a little urban jewel to pop in and out of

Rick's isn't exactly a hotel: it's a designer bar with ten contemporary rooms. When we arrived, we were a little confused about its status – who stays in bars, anyway? But walking into the lower-ground-floor bar, we were very pleasantly surprised. Low ceilings and coloured mood lighting give it a cosy, intimate atmosphere; brown banquette seats, burgundy leather cubes and giant cacti in stone pots make attractive surrounds. Classic house tunes play in the background, and the black-clad staff are friendly and obliging. It's modern, it's hip, it's bang in the middle of Edinburgh, and we've never been anywhere quite like it.

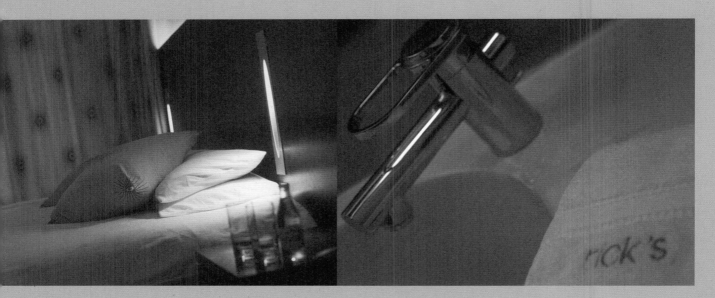

We passed by the open-plan kitchen to a door leading to the rooms above. They complement the bar extremely well; ours was simple but stylish, small but perfectly formed. There's no view, but all the mod cons were in place: CD, DVD, and an LCD TV with all the channels. In the well-stocked minibar we found a fun camera, Illy percolator, condoms and a toothbrush – we needn't have bothered to pack. Molton Brown toiletries and fluffy bathrobes are not what you'd expect for the price.

After a brasserie-style lunch downstairs, we felt we could afford to do a little shopping, since the room is so reasonable. And it would be rude not to see what Edinburgh has to offer. Harvey Nichols arrived a few years ago, and all the big-name stores and designers are no more than a few minutes' walk from the hotel.

Laden with bags, as the sun sets behind the beautiful backdrop of Edinburgh Castle, we set our hearts on a gin and tonic back at Rick's. Nothing makes me happier, when I'm staying in a city, than having a chic, central base as home for the weekend.

All thoughts of a G&T went out of the window when we saw the cocktail list; it is right up to the minute, and the bar staff at Rick's are seriously well trained. Mojitos all round. For dinner, we headed to popular rooftop restaurant Oloroso. Again, it is just round the corner (all that money saved on taxis – yet another excuse for rampant shopping), and entering it is like walking into a hip art gallery. It's on the fourth floor, with floor-to-ceiling windows giving spectacular views over the city to the sea.

A couple of bottles of wine later, we staggered up the road, to our own tuneless rendition of 'Danny Boy'. This brought us un-neatly to the sunken doorway of the Opal Lounge, where our names were on the door, thanks to the manager at Rick's. The rest is a blur; we fell headlong into a whisky-sampling session. We now felt more Scottish than Mel Gibson in *Braveheart* – if there had been a midnight kilt shop open, we'd have been there.

Breakfast is not included in the rate at Rick's, but that's probably a good thing. If you follow in our footsteps, you'll be lucky to make lunch. It makes a good spot to eat or drink any time of day, and transforms itself seamlessly, as the hours pass, from contemporary brasserie to sexy late-night bar, attracting the kind of unpretentious hipsters we love Edinburgh for. But what we'll be going back for is the concept of this little urban jewel to pop in and out of – Rick's owns some of the most inviting establishments in town, so you feel as though you've joined a sort of club for the weekend. Suddenly, New Year's Eve in Edinburgh seems a very good idea.

Reviewed by Mr & Mrs Smith

Need to know

Rooms Ten ensuite rooms.
Rates £110 (plus VAT).
Check-out 11am.
Facilities CDs and DVDs to borrow at the bar.
Kids Children welcome.

In the know

Recommended rooms 5, 8, 9 and 10 – although all the rooms are very similar.
Packing tips CDs and DVDs.

Food & drink

In the hotel A mix of Far Eastern and European dishes.
Dress code Urban chic.
Top table Conservatory seats are best in daytime; at night, go for a banquette.
Last orders Food: 10pm Sunday to Thursday; 11pm Friday and Saturday.
The bar is open 7am–1am.
Room service 24 hours.
Local restaurants **Oloroso** (0131 226 7614) is great for lunch and dinner. **Café St Honoré** (0131 226 2211), behind Rick's, is a good traditional French restaurant, as is **Atrium** (0131 228 8882). **Fishers** (0131 554 5666) serves fresh seafood down by the dock. Award-winning **Rhubarb** at Prestonfield (0131 668 3346) offers modern Scottish food using the best seasonal produce from Scotland's finest regional suppliers: Lindisfarne oysters, Isle of Skye scallops and Black Gold beef.
Local bars Rick's also owns the **Indigo Yard** (0131 220 5603), **Montpelier's** (0131 229 3115), **Assembly** (0131 220 4288) and the **Opal Lounge** (0131 226 2275). All serve food before transforming into DJ bars until 1am, except for the Opal Lounge, which shuts at 3am. If you're staying at Rick's, guestlists are not a problem.
Local pubs **Montpelier's** in Bruntsfield (0131 229 3115) is an Edinburgh institution for Sunday brunch. The **Cramond Inn** (0131 336 2035) is about four miles away, on the shore of the Firth of Forth.

Worth getting out of bed for

Shopping at Harvey Nicks, Jenners and George Street. A worthwhile trip out of town for whisky enthusiasts is Glenkinchie Distillery (01875 342004). Elie, near St Andrews, is a stunning beach about an hour's drive from Edinburgh (it won Best Beach in Britain 2003).
Diary August: Edinburgh International Festival (www.eif.co.uk); the Edinburgh Fringe Festival (www.edfringe.com); Edinburgh Film Festival (www.edfilmfest.org.uk).

Smith A complimentary cocktail and 15 per cent off your final bill in Rick's restaurant.

Get a room! Check availability and make reservations through www.mrandmrssmith.com.

Rick's 55a Frederick Street, Edinburgh (0131 622 7800)
info@ricksedinburgh.co.uk; www.ricksedinburgh.co.uk

The Witchery by the Castle

M T W T F █ M T W T F S S M T W T F S S M T W T F S S M T W T F S S M T W T

Style Historic opulence
Setting The foot of Edinburgh Castle

dinburgh

giant urns flank a bed half-obscured by cushions

Applause broke out as we touched down at Edinburgh airport. 50mph gusts of wind had left us a little shaken and we were delighted to get our feet on Scottish soil. We grabbed a cab into town and gazed from the windows at the magnificent history-steeped architecture of Scotland's first city. Driving up the Royal Mile, we wondered why on earth we had never visited Edinburgh before, and by the time we arrived at the foot of the fairy-tale castle we had become determined to get the most from our overnight stay.

A narrow path led us to the Witchery and at check-in we couldn't resist enquiring how the hotel got its name. Those hoping for a feelgood tale to accompany the inspiring surroundings, beware – the explanation is a bit more *The Crucible* than Hans Christian Andersen. Hundreds of witches were burned at the stake on Castlehill and this is where they had their last supper (sadly for them, whisky-cured salmon and grilled Scottish lobster had yet to make it onto the menu). As we were guided through a heavy wrought-iron gate, and up some narrow stone steps to our turret room, we started to wonder if maybe our all-black wardrobe had been misinterpreted, and we were to be locked up like those unfortunates all those centuries ago.

The truth is we would quite happily have been locked up for the night. The Vestry Suite is an opulent boudoir stuffed with antiques and ecclesiastical paraphernalia. Giant urns flank a bed half-obscured by cushions, with a headboard made of golden organ pipes. A crown and chandelier hang overhead, and we find a bottle of champagne waiting on ice next to a small selection of CDs by the hi-fi. At the touch of a button, a giant TV appears from a huge chest at the bottom of the bed.

Already lightheaded with excitement, we discover the 'secret' panelled doorway leading to the bathroom. A giant Victorian roll-top bath, velvet curtains, scented candles everywhere, a heated limestone floor – the 16th century this isn't. Even the most accomplished of the ladies who breathed their last but a stone's throw from this spot couldn't have conjured up more magical environs. A candlelit bath for two with bubbly in here and Laurence Llewellyn-Bowen would think he'd died and gone to heaven.

While we wouldn't have minded staying in our room all day and all night, it was time to see some more of Edinburgh. Part of the charm of the city centre is that you can wander around aimlessly, absorbing the incredible views in every direction. As we dawdled on Prince's Street, a dark cloud prompted us to head towards some umbrellas on offer for a fiver. Before we had the chance to reach into our wallets, the heavens opened and sent us running for cover to the nearest doorway – Jenner's, Edinburgh's answer to Selfridges. Not buying the brolly ended up a 'we might as well have a look around' which quickly turned into a £500 spending spree. Afterwards, in need of a dram, we went in search of the famous Cadenhead's Whisky Shop on Canongate. After the shopkeeper kindly let us sample his wares, we added a couple of 12-year-old malts to our haul and headed back to the Witchery before dinner.

We had a table reserved at one of the Witchery's three restaurants: the Tower, a five-minute cab ride away on the fifth floor of the Edinburgh Museum. With a view over the rooftops, the Tower was the perfect epilogue. Like the Secret Garden and Witchery restaurants, the more contemporary Tower is run with incredible attention to detail, and has an award-winning wine list.

As atmospheric and tempting as all three restaurants are, not even hunger could lure us out of the Vestry Suite in the morning. Instead, a heavily laden wicker trolley was delivered to our door. Not quite the last supper, but our last meal at the Witchery – for now.

Need to know

Rooms Seven suites, all packed with antiques and quirky collectibles.
Rates From £295, including breakfast, champagne and chocolates.
Check-out Midday.
Facilities Five suites have kitchenettes.
Kids We think you'll prefer it *à deux*.

In the know

Recommended rooms All are spectacular. We stayed in the Vestry Suite and loved it.
Packing tips Leave enough luggage space to take a couple of bottles of whisky home with you.
Also Expect to book a year ahead for weekends. Book car hire in advance if you want to escape the city: Avis have offices at the airport (0131 344 3900) and in the town centre (0131 337 6363).

Food & drink

In the hotel The Witchery is all wood panelling, candles and red leather. The Secret Garden is bigger and airier, with windows onto the terrace. Both serve contemporary Scottish food and are extremely romantic.
Dress code It's worthy of your finery.
Top table The Witchery: table 1. The Secret Garden: near the windows, or on the terrace in summer.
Last orders Lunch: 4pm; dinner: 11.30pm.
Room service No, but continental breakfast in bed is standard.
Breakfast 8am–10.30am.
Local restaurants **Fishers of Leith** (0131 554 5666) in the dock area is great for seafood.
The **Tower** (0131 225 3003), owned by the Witchery, is on the top floor of the Museum of Scotland.
Santini at the Sheraton (0131 221 7788) serves contemporary Italian food. Award-winning **Rhubarb** at Prestonfield (0131 668 3346) offers modern Scottish food using the best seasonal produce from Scotland's finest regional suppliers: Lindisfarne oysters, Isle of Skye scallops and Black Gold beef.
Local bars The **Opal Lounge** (0131 226 2275) open until 3am. **Rick's** (0131 622 7800; see page 266) for cocktails.
Local pubs For a pint in traditional surroundings, try the **Bow Bar** (0131 226 7667) on Victoria Street. The **Port O'Leith** (0131 554 3568) for a little edgy fun.

Worth getting out of bed for

Musselburgh Race Course, a winning racing setting (0131 665 2859; www.musselburgh-racecourse.co.uk) 'Ghosts and Gore' and 'Murder and Mystery' walks: tours start outside the hotel and are expertly presented (0131 225 6745; www.witcherytours.com). The view from Arthur's Seat in Holyrood Park is stunning, and the park provides a sanctuary from the city centre.
Diary August: Edinburgh International Festival (www.eif.co.uk); the Edinburgh Fringe Festival (www.edfringe.com); Edinburgh Film Festival (www.edfilmfest.org.uk). December: the legendary Edinburgh Hogmanay.

Get a room! Check availability and make reservations through www.mrandmrssmith.com.

The Witchery by the Castle Castlehill, The Royal Mile, Edinburgh (0131 225 5613)
mail@thewitchery.com; www.thewitchery.com

Scotland

Ireland

Wales

England

The Bell at Skenfrith

Tups indispensable

the white-painted former coaching inn has
been reincarnated as a comfortable and
restrained gastro hotel

M T W T F S S M T W T F S S M T W T F ■ M T W T F S S M T W T F S S M T W T

Style Peace in the valley
Setting Green, green grass of Monmouthshire

Skenfrith

Even in high summer, when the wind blows warm and zebra crossings become flirting opportunities for uptight city dwellers, Wales can mean rain. We were heading for Monmouthshire in order to leave all things townie behind; the Bell at Skenfrith was our get-out clause for the weekend, offering calm quiet, pastoral idyll, good food and, all things being usual, prodigious precipitation. With kagoules bundled in among the just-maybe shorts and halternecks, we fled the hustle and bustle.

We drove through ever hillier and more verdant landscape all the way to the Bell; the picture on the wittily designed brochure had us craning round every corner for the last five miles. In reality, its situation

couldn't be lovelier: it is tucked in between a swell in the gentle Welsh hills, the 13th-century castle of Skenfrith village and the river Monnow. The former coaching inn has been reincarnated as a comfortable and relaxed gastro hotel by William and Janet Hutchings, who bought it in 1999. Its history is there in the form of old village photos hanging on its white-painted walls; there are anecdotes to be had, mainly from fellow guests (we were held enthralled by a Chelsea wine merchant taking a break from tastings). The mainstay of the Bell is Janet, who treats her youthful staff like family. When we first arrived we found the service a little hesitant but, as they got used to us, the bar and restaurant staff showed themselves to be genuinely sweet and friendly. When we slipped out for a cigarette between courses on our first night, there was some mirth as to where we'd got to. In fact, we were

having a blissful look at the river, sitting on the old stone bridge with a companionable terrier, looking up a winding lane that had more than a touch of *Sleepy Hollow* to it.

In summer, the dining room and communal areas at the Bell are filled with intoxicatingly fresh flowers – armfuls of foxgloves greeted us on arrival. The pretty cottage garden at the back of the pub gives onto the tufty hedgerows of the local hills, which looked very enticing in the evening sun. In the morning, we borrowed a book and embarked, well-clad, on the 'Three Castles' walk. Think Lemon Jelly album cover, the folky goodness of *Led Zep III*, and livestock a-gogo – but do be warned: we came across No Boozers in this part of Wales. Do some homework, take some water, and arrange with Janet to pick you up from the second castle unless you are a hardcore walker. (We loved the caterpillars, buttercups, honeysuckle and dingly dells, but hitched a lift back to the Bell in a pick-up, gratefully ticking off the miles we would still have had to go). Ten miles over stiles and through copses did us nicely; Mr Smith fell on a pint of shandy when we got back to the hotel, and we sat speechlessly for some time before we went upstairs to dress for dinner.

One of the best things about our suite, Whickham's Fancy, was the sitting room; Mr Smith sat happily watching *Star Wars* while I soaked shamelessly for an hour, listening to Wagner. With so much time to be indulgent, I wished I'd brought some home-spa products to play with, to add to the Cath Collins goodies provided.

The food and wine at the Bell is a major draw; we both loved the Welsh black beef on the first night, and Mr Smith's tenderloin pork the next evening made him very happy indeed. We didn't see that much of the other guests; when we stayed up drinking Pineau de Charentes and malt whisky, we seemed to be the only Saturday night barflies in town. After heavy, healthy sleep, we bravely tackled more of the fine local produce at breakfast: eggs Florentine, smoked salmon and the full Welsh (black pudding, but they were out of brown sauce, to Mr Smith's dismay).

On Sunday, we didn't get nearly as far after breakfast; the Skenfrith Community Shop, with its Eighties knitting patterns, jam and five-pence bits and bobs, gave us a tantalising taste of village-fête-style preoccupations. Fishing, cycling, riding and hang-gliding could all have been arranged, but sticking around at the Bell made more sense. I'd probably put that down to the cosy bar, the wine list, of which they are rightly proud (there are some bargains to be had) – and the sheer thoughtfulness of the way the Hutchings run their beloved Bell.

Reviewed by Mr & Mrs Smith

Need to know

Rooms Eight.
Rates £100–£180, including breakfast.
Check-out 11am.
Facilities Widescreen TV with DVD player in each room.
Kids Extra beds and listening devices are available.
Also Smoking only allowed in the bar.

In the know

Recommended rooms Whickham's Fancy, the four-poster suite overlooking the river. Tups Indispensable, another four-poster. Coachman has a great view over the river and arched bridge.
Packing tips Walking boots, fishing rod and waterproofs. Home-spa products and an extensive selection of DVDs in case of bad weather.
Also Wellies and board games are provided. Pets are welcome.

Food & drink

In the hotel Modern British food, with a fantastic, good-value wine list.
Dress code Not too scruffy, not too sexy.
Top table 23 has the best view.
Last orders Food: 9.30pm; 9pm on Sundays. Guests can drink late in the bar.
Room service Continental breakfast in bed.
Breakfast 9am–10am.
Local restaurants The **Walnut Tree** in nearby Abergavenny (01873 852797) serves Italian food in rustic surroundings. The **Foxhunter** in Nantyderry near Usk (01873 881101) is one of Wales' most exciting new restaurants.
Local pubs The **Loughpool Inn**, at Sellack near Ross on Wye (01989 730236). Also worth the drive is the **Felin Fach Griffin** near Brecon (01874 620111), has great local produce.

Worth getting out of bed for

Incredible walks through stunning countryside: in particular, Yat Rock at Symonds Yat, for the views. Hang-gliding, cycling, canoeing, quad-biking, go-karting and archery can all be arranged by the hotel. This is also prime shooting-and-fishing country. Chepstow Racecourse, the premier Welsh track, is worth a visit (www.chepstow-racecourse.co.uk).
Diary March: Cheltenham Festival (01242 537642;www.cheltenham.co.uk). May: the Hay Festival of Literature (www.hayfestival.co.uk).

Smith A complimentary bottle of house champagne.

Get a room! Check availability and make reservations through www.mrandmrssmith.com.

The Bell at Skenfrith Skenfrith, Monmouthshire (01600 750235)
enquiries@skenfrith.com; www.skenfrith.com

Hurst House

MTWTF ◻ MTWTFSSMTWTFSSMTWT

Style Unexpected boutique hotel
Setting Lost in Wales

comfortable and lavish – an ideal getaway

East Marsh

Finding Hurst House is an adventure in its own right. We'd been on the road for hours, following instructions but feeling we were just driving deeper and deeper into the middle of Welsh nowhere. We had been expecting a contemporary hotel, but almost began to think we were losing our minds. We must have gone wrong somewhere: there just couldn't be a boutique hotel so far out in the wild, wild west. So we were relieved, to say the least when we saw little blue lights blinking through rock pillars scattered along the driveway – our first taste of Hurst. We ran to the front door through torrential rain, overjoyed to have found the place.

We were made to feel extremely welcome from the minute we arrived; our bags were picked up with a smile, and we were shown straight to our room. We thought at first that the hotel's look and feel appeared to follow a tried-and-trusted model of boho modern. Our room, however, was exceptional: a spacious split-level bedroom and living area in one of the converted outhouses (Hurst House is an old farm estate). The living area has an open fire – essential for all those rainy days – a chic leather sofa, and an impressive showing of Bang & Olufsen kit: TV, DVD player and stereo. The bit we loved best was the huge bathroom, with free-standing ball-and-claw bath, an enormous shower in the centre of the room, and fabulous black and white tiles.

We ate a couldn't-be-faulted late lunch in the bar, which has leather sofas to sink into, stacks of newspapers, a roaring fire and a good selection of wines and cocktails (not to mention friendly, attentive staff, who were a real laugh, too). And that was that. Without putting too fine a point on it, we spent the rest of the weekend being completely lazy and utterly selfish. The character and qualities of our room meant that we didn't really feel compelled to leave it too often. The weather also helped us decide on our stay-put strategy. The huge DVD library turned our den into a cinema, the staff waited on us hand and foot, the bed was heaven on four legs (big, with crisp White Company linen), and the bath was the kind that you lie in for hours, just lapping up the difference between 'having nothing much to do' and 'having nothing much to do somewhere

gorgeous'. Eating restaurant food in front of the fire is about as good as it gets in our eyes, though we did actually venture out to eat in the hotel restaurant for one dinner. What was especially good to see was the number of happy local faces in the restaurant and bar; it gave us a feeling of real atmosphere, and an extra 'discovery' feel to the hotel.

It isn't hard to imagine that, when it's not pouring, the countryside around Hurst House is breathtaking, but, frankly, in sheet rain, snuggling up in front of a good film with a glass of wine is more appealing by several miles. There are a number of Dylan Thomas-related attractions nearby – we visited the boathouse the celebrated soak wrote in, the beach that inspired him, and his house. There are other beaches that are good for lazy trudging, but you do have to drive to get to them. Five minutes from Hurst House is its owners' – Matt Roberts and actor Neil Morrissey – latest venture: the New Three Mariners pub. It has the air of a yacht club in Martha's Vineyard but they do a mean pint and pork pie.

We've got one word of warning about Hurst House – this haven will only appeal to the very idle and/or worn-out. You'll find books to read, DVDs to watch, log fires to loll by, delicious food to eat – but precious little else. If the rain pours down, however, outdoors is only an option for diehard enthusiasts, which makes Hurst House kind of perfect for lovers, too. The owners have plans for a health spa and a 30-seat cinema but, in the mean time, we'll be more than happy to check in, switch off and chill out.

Reviewed by Mr & Mrs Smith

Need to know

Rooms Seven; more in 2006.
Rates £125–£175, including breakfast.
Check-out Midday.
Kids Welcome, but not encouraged.
Also Smoking permitted, except in main dining room. Spa and treatment rooms opening in 2006.

In the know

Recommended rooms Room 106 is on two levels, with its own wood-burning stove for winter evenings.
Packing tips Welsh-English dictionary.

Food & drink

In the hotel A good selection of classic dishes using local ingredients.
Dress code Simple and snug.
Top table In the corner, tucked away.
Last orders Food: 10pm. Bar: as late as you'd like.
Room service 24 hours.
Breakfast 7.30am–11am.
Local restaurants The **Cors** (01994 427219) for fine dining. The **Portreeves** (01994 427476) is renowned for its home-cooked local recipes, and great for an intimate supper.
Local pubs The **New Three Mariners** (01994 427426) is a good place for a pint; **Brown's Hotel** (01994 427320) is where Dylan Thomas used to drink.

Worth getting out of bed for

The National Botanic Gardens in Aberglasney (01558 668768; www.gardenofwales.org.uk) nurtures endangered species from all over the world. A trip to Laugharne, a sleepy castle town on the Taff Estuary and poet Dylan Thomas' birthplace; you can see the boathouse where he wrote *Under Milk Wood*. The Welsh National Opera puts on concerts in Swansea (029 2046 4666; www.wno.org.uk). The beaches of Carmarthenshire Bay are only 15 miles away. Swiss Valley Reservoirs, near Llanelli (01554 752552) provides fly-fishing for brown and rainbow trout. A visit to Llundy Island can be arranged through Celtic Cruises (01446 734361; www.celticcruises.co.uk), which also offers other boating trips.
Diary August: the National Mud Festival of Wales, held at the Wetlands centre in Llanelli, is a weekend packed with mud safaris, mud sculptures, tug-of-war and welly-wanging competitions (01554 741087; www.wwt.org.uk).

Smith A bottle of champagne on arrival.

Get a room! Check availability and make reservations through www.mrandmrssmith.com.

Hurst House East Marsh, Laugharne, Carmarthenshire (01994 427417)
www.hurst-house.co.uk

how to use the diary

This is a calendar of established regular events around the UK and Ireland. We have provided the name of the event and the approximate timing. We have also given the organisers' contact details, so that you can find out the exact date for the year in question. The nearest *Mr & Mrs Smith* hotels are listed for each event.

Jan

Feb

Mar

Apr

May

Jun

Mr & Mrs Smith

Diary

Jul

Aug

Sep

Oct

Nov

Dec

In association with

MEMO: Make New Year's resolutions.

1 Jan – Cheltenham New Year Races (01242 537642; www.cheltenham.co.uk). National Hunt Racing. *The Bell, Cowley Manor*

– New Year's Day Dip, Whitley Bay, Tyne and Wear. Panama Swimming Club (club president Joe Carr – 0191 252 1623) swims in North Sea daily; they welcome many guests on New Year's Day for first swim of year. *Seaham Hall*

mid Jan – London International Boat Show, Excel, Docklands (01784 472222; www.londonboatshow.net). *Blakes*

MEMO: Remember to book for Valentine's Day.

MEMO: Three months until first spring bank holiday: book weekend away.

14 Feb – Valentine's Day.

early Mar – Bath Literary Festival (01225 463362; www.bathlitfest.org.uk). featuring likes of Fay Weldon, Ben Okri, Sebastian Faulkes. *Royal Crescent*

mid Mar – Cheltenham Festival: three days of hotly contested jump racing, including the Gold Cup (01242 537642; www.cheltenham.co.uk). *The Bell, Cowley Manor*

17 March – St Patrick's Day (+353 (0) 1 676 3205; www.stpatricksday.ie). Trip to Ireland. *Kilgraney, Morrison, TENsq*

Cheltenham Gold Cup (01242 537642; www.cheltenham.co.uk). *The Bell, Cowley Manor, Whatley Manor*

MEMO: Three months until summer: rejoin gym and book summer break.

early Apr – Grand National, Aintree, Liverpool (0151 523 2600; www.aintree.co.uk).

The most famous horse-race of them all, with notoriously high jumps.

Didsbury House

mid Apr – Glasgow Art Fair (0141 221 0049; www.glasgowartfair.com).

One Devonshire

_____

May – The Cat Laughs Comedy Festival – Ireland's version of the fringe

(+353 (0) 5663837; www.thecatlaughs.com). *Kilgraney*

– Brighton Festival (01273 709709; www.brighton-festival.org.uk).

England's answer to Edinburgh Fringe. *Blanch House, Hotel du Vin*

early May – Badminton Horse Trials (01454 218272; www.badminton-horse.co.uk).

Whatley Manor

mid May – Glyndebourne Opera (01273 813813; www.glyndebourne.com). Season

continues until end of August. *Amberley Castle*

– The Balmoral Show, Belfast (02890 665225; www.balmoralshow.co.uk)

Northern Ireland's premier Agricultural Show. *TENsq*

late May – Chelsea Flower Show (020 7649 1885; www.rhs.org.uk/chelsea). *Blakes*

– Prince's Polo, Windsor (www.princes-polo.co.uk). *Stoke Park*

– Coopers Hill Cheese Rolling Festival, Brockworth, Gloucestershire

(www.cheese-rolling.co.uk). *Cotswold House Hotel*

May/June – The Hay Festival of Literature (www.hayfestival.co.uk). *The Bell*

Cartmel Steeplechase Races (www.cartmel-steeplechases.co.uk). *L'Enclume*

Longleat International Horse Trials, Longleat House, Warminster (01404

MEMO: Six months until New Year's – book a hotel.

early June – Epsom Derby, (01372 470047; www.epsomderby.co.uk). *Blakes*

Mid June – Royal Ascot, inc Ladies Day (01344 622211; www.ascot.co.uk). *Stoke Park*

– Barrow Grand Prix Barrow Docks, Lake District (01228 562483; www.wmbrc-racing.net). *L'Enclume, the Samling*

– The Royal Norfolk Show: sheepdogs etc (01603 748931; www.royalnorfolkshow.co.uk). *Ickworth, Strattons, the Victoria*

– The Windsor International Horse Trials (01993 813794; www.windsorhorsetrials.com). *Le Manoir aux Quat' Saisons*

late June – Round the Island Race, Cowes, Isle of Wight (01983 296621; www.islandsc.org.uk). *Onion Store, Westover Hall*

– Wimbledon Lawn Tennis Championships, London SW19 (020 8944 1066; www.wimbledon.org). *Blakes, Covent Garden Hotel, Portobello*

– Northumberland Plate Festival (0191 236 2020; www.newcastle-racecourse.co.uk). *Seaham Hall*

– Polo British Open Championships (01730 813257; www.cowdraypolo.co.uk). Three weeks of polo tournaments. *Amberley Castle, Royal Oak*

– Henley Royal Regatta (01491 572153; www.hrr.co.uk) – Five-day rowing meet. *Cotswold House, Le Manoir, Stoke Park*

– The Royal Highland Show near Edinburgh (0131 335 6200; www.royalhighlandshow.org). *Rick's, the Witchery*

July — The Veuve Clicquot Gold Cup Final, Cowdray Park Polo Club (01730 813257; www.cowdraypolo.co.uk). *Amberley Castle, Royal Oak*

— Royal Ascot (01344 622211; www.ascot.co.uk). *Stoke Park*

— Glorious Goodwood (01243 755022; www.goodwood.co.uk). *Amberley, Royal Oak*

— Rip Curl Newquay Boardmasters, Cornwall (BSA 01637 851487; www.britsurf.co.uk). *Driftwood, the Lugger, Hotel Tresanton*

— Farnborough International Airshow, Surrey (020 7227 1043; www.farnborough.com). World's largest airshow. *Stoke Park*

— World Offshore Powerboat Championship, Plymouth (020 7349 7623; www.class-1.com). *Burgh Island*

— Sunderland International Kite Festival (01923 822085). *Seaham Hall*

— Royal International Air Tattoo, RAF Fairford (01285 713300; www.airtattoo.com). *Barnsley House*

— Gairloch Sheepdog Trials (01445 712412). *Pool House*

— Oxygen Music Festival (www.oxygen.ie). *Morrison*

— Newmarket Nights (www.newmarketnights.co.uk). *Ickworth*

— Ryedale Festival (01751 475777; www.ryedalefestival.co.uk). *Star Inn*

— Garsington Opera (01865 361636; www.garsingtonopera.org). *Le Manoir*

— Great Yorkshire Show (01423 541222; www.greatyorkshireshow.org). *Star Inn*

— Round the Island Race, Cowes (01983 296621; www.islandsc.org.uk). *Westover Hall*

early-mid July — British Grand Prix, Silverstone (01327 850211; www.silverstone-circuit.co.uk).

mid July — Festival of Speed, Goodwood (01243 755022; www.goodwood.co.uk). *Amberley Castle, Royal Oak*

mid July-Sept — The Proms, Royal Albert Hall (020 7589 8212; www.bbc.co.uk/proms).

mid-late July — British Classic Yacht Regatta (01983 293581) at the Royal Corinthian Yacht Club, Cowes. *Onion Store, Westover Hall*

late July — Cartier International Polo, Windsor Great Park (01784 434212; www.guardspoloclub.com). *Stoke Park*

Aug – British surfing Championships, Newquay

(www.surfnewquay.co.uk). *The Lugger*

– Assynt Highland Games Culag Park, Lochinver (01571 844647;

www.albagames.co.uk). *Pool House*

– Duck Race: hundreds of rubber ducks are floated down the river in

biannual river madness. *Pool House*

– Castle Howard Proms (0845 2256020; www.castlehoward.co.uk). *Star Inn*

– The British Horse Trials Championships, Gatcombe Park

(01460 281 545). *Whatley Manor*

Edinburgh – Three festivals, all month: Edinburgh International Festival – 'main' festival

of high-profile events (www.eif.co.uk); Edinburgh Fringe Festival – hundreds

of smaller shows inc comedy (www.edfringe.com); Edinburgh Film Festival

(www.edfilmfest.org.uk). *Ricks, the Witchery*

early Aug – Glastonbury Festival (01458 832020;

www.glastonburyfestivals.co.uk/classical). Glastonbury for grown-ups –

normally classical, in 2003 Jools Holland and Orchestra)

– Cowes Week (01983 295744; www.cowesweek.co.uk). Yachting

spectacular, fab fireworks Friday night. *Onion Store, Westover Hall*

– International Balloon Fiesta, Long Ashton, Bristol (0117 953 5884;

www.bristolfiesta.co.uk). *Babington House*

mid Aug – Falmouth Regatta (01326 211555; www.pofsa.org). *Driftwood, Tresanton*

late Aug – Blackpool Illuminations (www.blackpooltourism.com) alight until Nov.

– Notting Hill Carnival (020 8964 0544; www.thecarnival.tv). Largest

carnival in northern hemisphere. Spectacular multicultural feast,

Caribbean-style. *Portobello*

– Grasmere Sports and Show (01539 435245; www.grasmeresports.co.uk)

Largest show in the Lakes. *Drunken Duck, L'Enclume, The Samling*

Sept — Blenheim International Horse Trials, Blenheim Palace (01993 811325; www.blenheimpalace.com). *Cotswold House, Le Manoir*

early Sept — Great River Race (020 8398 9057; www.greatriverrace.co.uk). Over 250 'traditional' boats vie over the 22-mile course from Richmond to Greenwich. *Blakes, Covent Garden Hotel*

mid Sept — Southampton Boat Show (0115 912 9190; www.southamptonboatshow.com). *Onion Store, Westover Hall*

— 'Animal' Poole Windfest, Dorset (01202 707757; www.poolewindfest.co.uk). Windsurfing and kite surfing displays and competition. *Westover Hall*

mid-late Sept — London Open House (0900 160 0061; www.londonopenhouse.org). Free access to buildings of architectural and cultural interest that are normally closed to the public. *Covent Garden Hotel, Portobello*

Oct — Windermere Powerboat Records (01539 443284; www.rya.org.uk/powerboating). *Drunken Duck, L'Enclume, the Samling*

— Champion's Day at Newmarket (www.newmarketracecourses.co.uk). *Ickworth, Strattons, the Victoria*

— Wexford Opera Festival (+353 (0) 53 22144; www.wexfordopera.com).

Late Oct — Zapcat Championship Final, location tbc (02380 222262; www.zapcat-racing.com).

MEMO: Three months until Valentine's Day – book romantic retreat.

5 Nov –   Guy Fawkes Night: bonfires and fireworks all over the country.

mid Nov –   London Christmas lights and tree. Each year, a giant fir-tree takes up

residence in Trafalgar Square, with ceremonial switching-on of lights

and carol singing. *Blakes, Covent Garden Hotel, Portobello*

– London Film Festival (020 7928 3535; www.lff.org.uk). Attracts

big-name actors and directors – a chance to see new films at

decent prices. *Blakes, Covent Garden Hotel, Portobello*

late Nov –   Hennessy Gold Cup (01635 40015; www.newbury-racecourse.co.uk).

Stoke Park

Nov/Dec –   Ice-skating at Somerset House (020 7836 8686;

www.somerset-house.org.uk). *Blakes, Covent Garden Hotel, Portobello*

_____

late Dec-Jan –   Harrods Winter Sale, London (020 7730 1234; www.harrods.com).

Blakes, Covent Garden, Portobello

31 Dec –   Hogmanay, Edinburgh. *Rick's, The Witchery*

Dec –   Welsh National Racing, Chepstow (01291 622260;

www.chepstow-racecourse.co.uk). *The Bell*

_____

NB: event details can change.

Please check with the organisers that the event is happening before

making travel arrangements. Read our disclaimer.

pack it in

Backgammon set
Batteries
Beach towel
Binoculars
Books/mags
Bottle of Mercier champagne
Camcorder
Camera/film
Cards
CDs
Condoms
Cool-box
Corkscrew
DVDs/videos
Erotica
Flip-flops
Frisbee
Hangover cures
Hat, scarf and gloves
Home-spa products
Kite
Massage oil
Mobile-phone charger
Myla lingerie and toys
Ordnance Survey map
Picnic hamper
Picnic rug
Polaroid camera
Portable CD player
Rizlas
Scented candles
Scrabble
Suncream
Sunglasses
Swimming costume
Swiss Army knife
Umbrella
Wellingtons
Walking boots

(useful numbers)

Gran Turismo (0131 466 3447; www.granturismo.demon.co.uk) provides Scotland, Newcastle and the Lakes with luxury classic cars, sports cars and 4x4s.

The Open Road (01926 624 891; www.theopenroad.co.uk) in Warwickshire has Triumphs, MG-Bs and Jaguars.

Erotica

Myla (08707 455003; www.myla.com) is celebrated for its seductive and stunning lingerie, designer sex toys and jewellery, as well as own-brand herbal aphrodisiac products. Myla will deliver any order over £50 to any of the hotels featured in *Mr & Mrs Smith*, free of charge – an exclusive offer.

Ooshka (0800 3286231; www.ooshka.com) is great for funky bedroom toys, playful sexcessories, lingerie, unusual aphrodisiacs and sensual bath and massage products.

Events

Lastminute.com has some great suggestions, and can provide last-minute tickets to events around the UK.

Ticketmaster (0870 534 4444; www.ticketmaster.co.uk) does tickets for theatre, music and sporting events.

Helicopters and private-plane hire

Air Charter Scotland (0131 339 8008) is based at Edinburgh Airport.

Elite Helicopters (www.elitehelicopters.co.uk) operates from White Waltham (01628 828188) in Berkshire and Goodwood Airfield near Chichester (01243 530165).

Evolution in London (0871 222 1974; www.my-skys.com) takes passengers up the Thames from Battersea to the Thames Barrier.

Fly Ireland in North County Dublin (+353 (0)184 15261; www.flyirl.com) specialises in executive aircraft charter.

Northern Executive Aviation (0161 436 6666) is based at Manchester airport.

Polo Aviation (01934 877000) in Bristol has both planes and helicopters for charter and pleasure flights.

Maps

Streetmap (www.streetmap.co.uk) pinpoints any UK location on a map. **AA Routefinder** helps you find the best routes in the UK and Ireland (www.theaa.com).

Tourist organisations

The National Trust (0870 458 4000; www.nationaltrust.org.uk). **British Tourist Authority** (www.visitbritain.com).

Trains

For train tickets and timetables, go to www.thetrainline.com, or try **National Rail Enquiries** (08457 484950; www.nationalrail.co.uk).

SO, WHO ARE MR & MRS SMITH?

Right from the start, we knew it was important to give you an honest account of what you can expect when you visit a *Mr & Mrs Smith* hotel. In order to really give you the insider information, we selected a panel of people who we feel are credible, and who can see in the dark when it comes to style, fun and originality. They all reviewed the hotels anonymously, so there was no special treatment. What you read is actually what happened on their *Mr & Mrs Smith* trip. The only obligation was that they went with a partner and brought us back the kind of honest account you would expect to get from your best friend.

THE ARCHITECT

Anthony Thistleton established the architectural practice Waugh Thistleton with Andrew Waugh six years ago, just when Shoreditch was emerging from hibernation. Anthony and Andrew became an integral part of the area's regeneration, setting up in shopfront premises and offering advice to all callers. Their local work includes Cantaloupe and the Light Bar and, more recently, the Eyre Brothers restaurant. Further afield, they designed the White House in Clapham, the Waterway in Maida Vale and the Northern Light in Leeds. The practice now numbers 14 partners; projects range from artists' studios to large-scale residential and commercial developments.

THE BAR OWNER

Born in Hong Kong, **Eric Yu** moved to London at the age of three. He studied economics at Leeds, then trained and qualified as a chartered accountant before joining a leisure company as financial controller. Leaving the company in 1991, along with the colleague who became his business partner, he purchased London nightclub Villa Stefano, and then built on its success by transforming Jimmy's Bar into Bar Rumba. Eric's Breakfast Group (named for the wee small hours his business thrives during) now includes the Substations, Jerusalem, Social, POP, Social Nottingham, Opium and Grand Central. In 2002, *Theme* magazine named Eric Yu most influential individual in the industry.

THE CHEF

Born in Besançon, France in 1949, **Raymond Blanc** is acknowledged as one of the finest chefs in the world. His cuisine has been described as intelligent, daring, imaginative and adventurous, and he has received tributes from every national and international guide to culinary excellence. In 1984, he opened Le Manoir aux Quat' Saisons in Great Milton, Oxford, and fulfilled his personal vision of creating a hotel and restaurant in harmony, where guests can expect perfection in cuisine, service and comfort. Le Manoir is the only country-house hotel in the UK to maintain two Michelin stars for 16 years.

THE CLUB OWNER

Rory Keegan is the founder and creator of Chinawhite and Taman Gang in London, and the Mao Rooms in Ibiza. He spends his time designing nightclubs throughout the world and is currently engaged in creating a club in Moscow. In past lives he has been involved in fine art at Sotheby's, microlight aircraft in Wales, feature films in LA and theatre in the West End of London. His big hit was *Les Liaisons Dangereuses*, reputedly inspired by his rather strange personal life.

THE MAGAZINE EDITORS

Tiffanie Darke is editor of *The Sunday Times Style* magazine. She is also an author, and has published two novels: *Marrow*, a saucy tale of food and sex in the kitchens of London's celebrity restaurants, and *Strapline*, a story of celebrity, football, and love on a national newspaper. She considers herself an expert on dirty weekends.

After being hired and fired from a series of highly unsuitable jobs, **Phil Gould** returned to education and earned a bachelor's degree in communications. His first foray into journalism proper came as a cub reporter on the *Scunthorpe Evening Telegraph*, where he eventually became deputy news editor. A nomadic existence at a number of regional newspapers ended when he arrived at the Press Association's London headquarters to become showbusiness features editor. He is currently news editor at *OK!* magazine.

After graduating from Central St Martins, **Jeremy Langmead** fell into journalism when he accepted a job as a sub-editor on *Mirabella* magazine without knowing what a sub-editor was. He is now editor-in-chief of the style bible *Wallpaper**. Before that, he edited the Life & Style pages of the *Evening Standard*, followed by the relaunched *Nova* and, for six years, was editor of *The Sunday Times Style* magazine. He has written for numerous mags and newspapers, such as *Elle Decoration*, *GQ*, *The Guardian* and *The Independent*.

After coming to the attention of the music press for his fanzine, **Anthony Noguera** edited various music magazines in the Nineties before joining *Sky* as a senior features writer in 1993. He joined *FHM* as features editor in 1995, and became editor in April 1999. He edited the magazine until September 2001. Under his editorship, it became the bestselling monthly in British history; it also gave Jennifer Lopez her first ever cover story. He was made EMAP Editor of the Year in 1999; and British Society of Magazine Editors Editor of the Year in 2000. Anthony moved to *Arena* as editor-in-chief in October 2001.

Matt Turner is the editor of *Sleeper*, the UK's leading hotel-design magazine. He studied journalism in Liverpool in the early Nineties, but spent most of his time in nightclubs. He then joined Mondiale Publishing as a trainee on *Night* magazine. He became editor within three years, and travelled extensively during the next five years to clubs throughout the UK. His role involved visits to party capitals such as Paris, Rimini, Milan, Ibiza, Miami, Las Vegas and New York, staying in hotels of all shapes and sizes. In September 2002, he was appointed editor of *Sleeper*. He now spends even more time checking out contemporary hotels in all their guises, and gets a lot more sleep than he used to.

Lucy Yeomans began her career in 1993 in Paris, where she was editor of an English-language lifestyle monthly. She also freelanced for *Harpers & Queen* and *The Sunday Times*. Returning to the UK, she was appointed features editor of *The European*, and moved to *Tatler* in 1997 as features editor, becoming deputy editor a year later. At lunchtime on her first day as features director of British *Vogue*, she was offered, and accepted, the position of editor at *Harpers & Queen*. That was in November 2000; since then, Lucy has transformed *Harpers* into one of the world's most chic and talked-about magazines.

THE FASHION DESIGNER

Tracey Boyd is the designer behind the modern British womenswear label Boyd, which expanded out of her back bedroom in the late Nineties. At Boyd's first catwalk show in 1999, Fatboy Slim was there mixing the music live, and in February 2000, Tracey won the New Generation prize at the British Fashion Awards, having been nominated alongside Stella McCartney. The first Boyd shop opened in September 2001, exactly five years after the company was founded, at 42 Elizabeth Street in London's Belgravia, and the label continues to expand around the world.

THE GALLERY OWNER

Alexander Proud founded Proud Galleries after incarnations as an antiques dealer, an oriental-gallery owner and an Internet pioneer. He made his reputation with shows such as 'Destroy – the Sex Pistols'. Subsequent shows, including Rankin's 'Nudes' project, have cemented the position of Proud Galleries as one of the most exciting photographic galleries in Europe. He sits on the panels of various photographic bodies, and is a guest commenter for the BBC. 2001 saw the launch and success of Proud Camden Moss, and further launches are planned in Brighton, New York, Paris and Tokyo.

THE JOURNALIST

Chris Elwell-Sutton started off writing for *Dazed & Confused* and *Hip Hop Connection* magazines while he was at Edinburgh University. Chris worked for *Smash Hits*, and was deputy editor of clubbing magazine *Ministry*, before a year editing dance-music title *Muzik*. Since then, he has written for the *Evening Standard*, *The Times*, *Esquire* and *FHM*, to name but three, and he is now deputy editor of the *Evening Standard*'s *Metro Life* magazine.

THE MUSIC PRODUCER

Following eight years in advertising, **Ben Sowton** co-founded the successful events company Atomic, producing shows, conferences and tours in the UK and abroad, for an international client list that included Ralph Lauren, Bacardi-Brown Forman and 100% Design. Three years ago, he co-founded the White House members' bar and restaurant in South London. He then fulfilled a long-held ambition to set up a record label, Seamless Recordings, whose *bargrooves*, a house-music compilation series, has been described by *Wallpaper** as 'achingly sophisticated'.

THE PR

American-born **Jori White** set up her PR consultancy in 1995, with clients including the Anse Chastanet hotel in St Lucia, and the Etrusca Group of nine restaurants, including Il Convivio, the Cinnamon Club and Zuma. All have enjoyed unprecedented good publicity, resulting in increased turnovers. Jori White PR also represents Table Talk, London's finest food design and events company, which organised the Mario Testino launch at the National Portrait Gallery in London, and threw *Tatler*'s 100 Most Invited party last year.

THE PUBLISHER

In 1987, **Elaine Foran** was a graduate trainee at *The Independent*; the next year, she was headhunted to work on the *Evening Standard*, and the launch of *ES*. In 1989, she moved to the Express Group, and then in 1992 to *New Woman*. At 26 she became publisher of *Elle*, and months after being appointed international publisher for EMAP Elan, she became publisher of *Nova* at IPC. Elaine has been fashion and international publishing director for IPC, for titles such as *Marie Claire*, *Living Etc* and *InStyle*, since 2001.

THE RETAILER

Oliver Tress is the brains behind the Oliver Bonas chain of stores, which sells lifestyle products, from clothing to contemporary furniture. Since its launch in November 1993, Oliver Bonas has opened more than ten shops across London. Oliver developed his passion for retail in his days as an importer of fashion goods from Hong Kong, initially catering for friends' demands. His plans for the future are focused on international expansion and the development of branded product lines, such as a jewellery range.

THE ROCK STAR

Felix Buxton is one half of Basement Jaxx, the dance-music duo who showed us, with debut album *Remedy*, that basslines, classic tunes and star quality aren't mutually incompatible. Felix and his musical partner Simon Ratcliffe fuse Latin, ragga and hip hop with the underground sounds and attitude of their native South London. They stormed Glastonbury in 2000 with a riot of flamenco dancers, MCs, singers and somersaulting percussionists, and they've taken the sound of SW9 to Australia, America and Japan. They started up the word-of-mouth Rooty nights in a pub, with Felix designing the flyers and painting the banners himself, and in 2001 they released their fantastic follow-up LP of the same name. In October 2003 they gave us *Kish Kash*.

THE TV PRODUCER

Stephanie Dennis is a freelance producer/director who started her TV career making cups of tea for Chris Evans on *The Big Breakfast* when it launched in 1992. Fortunately she was rubbish at making tea, and moved on up into the world of top-notch tacky TV, directing *Blind Dates* for Cilla, grilling the contestants on *Gladiators*, and searching for *Pop Idols*. Her career has taken her around the globe and, most recently, Shepherd's Bush, where she is senior producer on Sky One's *Fear Factor*.

THE MR & MRS SMITH TEAM

James Lohan is one half of the couple behind *Mr & Mrs Smith*. James' first company, Atomic, created the infamous Come Dancing parties and club promotions. (One of his London parties, in 1998, was voted 'number-one place to be in the world' by *FHM*.) He built on this success with Atomic Events and Atomic Promotions with Ben Sowton, producing events for clients such as Jack Daniel's, Finlandia vodka and Wonderbra. He then went on to co-found the White House bar, restaurant and members' club in Clapham. Launched in March 2000, it is one of London's hippest establishments.

Tamara Heber-Percy, the co-founder of *Mr & Mrs Smith*, graduated from Oxford with a degree in languages, then left the UK for a year in Brazil, where she launched a new energy drink. Since then, she has worked as a marketing consultant for international brands such as Ericsson, Honda, Unilever and Swissair. Her last role in that field was in business-development for Europe, Middle East and Africa at one of the UK's top marketing agencies. She left the corporate world in 2002 to head up her own company – an exclusive introductions agency – but still takes on consultancy projects, the most recent at an inflight-entertainment media company.

Bloom Design, the creators of the Mr & Mrs Smith brand and designers of the book – are one of the UK's freshest design agencies. Founded by three of the youngest heavyweights in the industry in 2001 – Gavin Blake, Ben White and Harriet Marshall – they are responsible for inspirational brand designs for some of Europe and the USA's leading consumer-brand companies. Their house style is bold, iconic and distinctive and their attitude open and irreverent. The Bloom team on *Mr & Mrs Smith* are director Ben White, senior account manager Oona Bannon, senior designer Samantha Armes, designer Emily Wood and production director Tim Reynolds.

Editor **Juliet Kinsman** cut her teeth as editor of the *UK Club Guide*. Having garnered an in-depth knowledge of who was playing what records in the early Nineties, she is looking forward to the invention of the necessary neurotechnology to let her replace it with something more useful. Over the past decade Juliet has written for *Time Out*, *The Face*, *The Guardian*, *Marie Claire*, *Condé Nast Traveller* and the BBC. A spell reviewing hotels and restaurants for TV stole her a behind-the-scenes look at the industry.

Editor **Sophie Dening** graduated from UCL in 1997 and spent a brief idyll at a business and academic publisher in North London, before finding her way onto the subs desk at *Tatler* magazine in 1999, where she learnt everything there is to know about pearls, polo and Prada. Since 2001, Sophie has been chief sub-editor at *Harpers & Queen*, where she also writes the books page.

Publisher **Andrew Grahame** launched the first title dedicated to corporate fashion in 1987. After setting up fashion shows, exhibitions and conferences, Andrew became director of Aquarius Publishing, launching *Small Company Investor*. In 1993, he created the events-production company GP Promotions, with clients such as Sony, Virgin, Evian and Paco Rabanne. In 1997, he founded the Leisure Pass Group, behind both the London Pass and the New York Pass. The London Pass won the English Tourism Council's Excellence in Marketing Award 2002 and is the most advanced tourism pass of its kind.

After his degree, photographer **Adrian Houston** embarked on a practical education, becoming assistant to Michael Joseph, one of the UK's leading commercial photographers. Adrian has worked with some of the industry's top advertising agencies, including Saatchi & Saatchi, JWT and Leo Burnett. He went on to add portraiture and landscape photography to his advertising and fashion portfolios, and has since been commissioned to photograph famous faces including the Dalai Lama, Sir Ranulf Fiennes, Luciano Pavarotti and Jim Carrey.

After graduating from Oxford with a degree in modern languages, **Emma Webley** gained first-hand experience of what delivering excellent experiences is all about during her first job, working for Raymond Blanc. She has since worked for George Soros, and for Justgiving, an internet charity donation website, and in television production. Emma took on the role of senior production manager at Spy Publishing to help make *Mr & Mrs Smith* a reality, and is looking forward to finally using her languages for a subsequent Smith publication, when the couple venture overseas.

Edward Orr entered the world of investment banking in 1992, and worked on a number of European corporate-finance transactions. In 1998 he became a vice-president of BT Alex Brown, but soon decided to head to business school in Barcelona for two years. After helping a new Austrian company raise £40 million from Deutsche Telekom, he went on to do the same for the UK launch of uboot, to the tune of £5 million. Since then, Edward has been working for an investment-banking boutique specialising in emerging technologies, as well as finding time to be finance director of *Mr & Mrs Smith* – definitely his most enjoyable venture so far.

[applause]

thank you

This book would never have made it onto the shelves without the hard work and creativity of our team. Thank you to publishing director Andrew Grahame, for his guidance and inspiration; Adrian Houston, for his stunning photography; editors Juliet Kinsman and Sophie Dening for their exceptional way with words; senior production manager Emma Webley for her skill and dedication; finance director Edward Orr, for keeping us on track; Bloom Design, for their vision and originality, with special thanks to Samantha Armes, Oona Bannon, John Cox, Harriet Marshall, Tim Reynolds, Ben White and Emily Wood; Jori White, Irena Pogarcic, Jonny Lockwood and Rachael Oliveck for letting you know about us; Rick Webb for the beautiful website; Edward Gretton; Hallmark, for getting the books to you; Portfolio Distribution and its sales team, with special thanks to Hugh Brune, Charles Arnold, Veronica Bromley and Carol Farley; the hotels, for recognising our vision; the reviewers, for giving us the inside track; our investors, for believing in us; the shops that stock us; Tsunami Creative; and Trichrom Ltd for printing the book. A big thank-you to Mercier champagne; Myla, for the sexiest lingerie money can buy; Dunhill for supplying beautiful accessories; and Nelson Design and Zoffany. Thanks also to photography assistants Alex Salkeld and Tom Mattey; Hasselblad cameras; Blakes for the front cover; Marcus Black from TAOTM; Alex Duckworth; Max Crane-Robinson; Danielle Rigby; Ben Illis; Kate Taylor; Rob Milton; Olly Phillips; Jay Woods; Laura Fowler; and all the 'other halves' who went away to review a hotel with their partners, or helped with the content.

Mr & Mrs Smith